GUINNESS WORLD RECORDS 2017

BLOCK BUSTERS!

OFFICIALLY AMAZING

British Library
Cataloguing-in-publication data: a catalogue record for this book is available from the British Library.

ISBN:
UK: 978-1-910561-49-2
US 10: 1-910561-50-9
US 13: 978-1-910561-50-8
Can: 978-1-897553-52-7

Records are made to be broken – indeed, it is one of the key criteria for a record category – so if you find a record that you think you can beat, tell us about it by making a record claim. Find out how on page 6. Always contact us before making a record attempt.

Guinness World Records does not claim to own any right, title or interest in any third party intellectual property reproduced in this book.

For picture credits, please refer to page 214.

Check the official website – **www.guinnessworld records.com** – regularly for record-breaking news, plus video footage of record attempts. You can also join and interact with the Guinness World Records online community.

Sustainability
The paper used for this edition is manufactured by UPM Plattling, Germany. The production site has forest certification and its operations have both ISO14001 environmental management system and EMAS certification to ensure sustainable production.

UPM Papers are true Biofore products, produced from renewable and recyclable materials.

BLOCKBUSTERS! 2017

PROJECT EDITOR (LEAD)
Adam Millward

EDITOR-IN-CHIEF
Craig Glenday

SENIOR MANAGING EDITOR
Stephen Fall

PROJECT EDITOR
Ben Hollingum

GAMING EDITOR
Stephen Daultrey

INFORMATION & RESEARCH MANAGER
Carim Valerio

HEAD OF PICTURES & DESIGN
Michael Whitty

DEPUTY PICTURE EDITOR
Fran Morales

PICTURE RESEARCHER
Wilf Matos

TALENT RESEARCHERS
Jenny Langridge, Victoria Tweedy

ORIGINAL PHOTOGRAPHY
Paul Michael Hughes, James Ellerker

VP PUBLISHING
Jenny Heller

DIRECTOR OF PROCUREMENT
Patricia Magill

PUBLISHING MANAGER
Jane Boatfield

PRODUCTION ASSISTANT
Thomas McCurdy

DESIGN
Flawless: Keren Turner, Robert Burdick, Kevin Baker

ARTWORKER
Billy Waqar

PRINTING & BINDING
MOHN Media Mohndruck GmbH, Gütersloh, Germany

PRODUCTION CONSULTANTS
Roger Hawkins, Dennis Thon

REPROGRAPHICS
Res Kahraman, Born Group

PROOFREADER
Matthew White

INDEXER
Marie Lorimer

CORPORATE OFFICE
Global President: Alistair Richards

Professional Services
Chief Financial Officer: Alison Ozanne
Financial Controller: Andrew Wood
Accounts Receivable Manager: Lisa Gibbs
Finance Managers: Jaimie-Lee Emrith, Daniel Ralph
Assistant Accountant: Jess Blake
Accounts Payable Assistant: Victoria Aweh
Accounts Payable Clerk: Tajkiya Sultana
Trading Analysis Manager: Elizabeth Bishop
Head of Legal & Business Affairs: Raymond Marshall
Solicitor: Terence Tsang
Legal & Business Affairs Executive: Xiangyun Rablen
Paralegal: Michelle Phua
Head of HR: Farrella Ryan-Coker
HR Assistant: Mehreen Saeed
Office Manager: Jackie Angus
Director of IT: Rob Howe
IT Development Manager: James Edwards
Developer: Cenk Selim
Junior Developer: Lewis Ayers
Desktop Administrator: Alpha Serrant-Defoe
SVP Records: Marco Frigatti
Head of Category Management: Jacqui Sherlock / Shantha Chinniah
Information & Research Manager: Carim Valerio
RMT Training Manager: Alexandra Popistan
Records Managers: Sam Golin, Corrinne Burns, Adam Brown, Tripp Yeoman, Victoria Yeoman
Records Consultants: Sam Mason, Tom Ibison

Global Brand Strategy
SVP Global Brand Strategy: Samantha Fay

Global Product Marketing
VP Global Product Marketing: Katie Forde
Director of Global TV Content & Sales: Rob Molloy
Senior TV Distribution Manager: Paul Glynn

Senior TV Content Executive: Jonathon Whitton
Digital Product Marketing Manager: Veronica Irons
Online Editor: Kevin Lynch
Online Writer: Rachel Swatman
Social Media Manager: Dan Thorne
Digital Video Producer: Matt Musson
Front-End Developer: Alex Waldu
Brand & Consumer Product Marketing Manager: Lucy Acfield
Designer: Rebecca Buchanan Smith
Junior Designer: Edward Dillon
Product Marketing Assistant: Victor Fenes

EMEA & APAC
SVP EMEA APAC: Nadine Causey
VP Creative: Paul O'Neill
Attractions Development Manager: Louise Toms
PR Director: Jakki Lewis
Senior PR Manager: Doug Male
Senior Publicist: Madalyn Bielfeld
B2B PR Manager: Melanie DeFries / Juliet Dawson
UK & International Press Officer: Amber-Georgina Gill
Head of Marketing: Justine Tommey / Chriscilla Philogene
Senior B2B Marketing Manager: Mawa Rodriguez
B2C Marketing Manager: Christelle Betrong
Content Marketing Executive: Imelda Ngouala
Head of Publishing Sales: John Pilley
Licensing Manager, Publishing: Emma Davies
Key Accounts Manager: Caroline Lake
Distribution Executive: Alice Oluyitan
Head of Commercial Accounts & Licensing: Sam Prosser
Business Development Manager: Mark Kelly
Commercial Account Managers: Lucie Pessereau, Jessica Rae, Inga Rasmussen, Sadie Smith
Commercial Account Executive: Fay Edwards
Commercial Representative, India: Nikhil Shukla
Country Manager, MENA: Talal Omar

Head of RMT, MENA: Samer Khallouf
Records Manager, MENA: Hoda Khachab
B2B Marketing Manager, MENA: Leila Issa
Commercial Account Manager, MENA: Khalid Yassine
Head of Records Management, Europe & APAC: Ben Backhouse
Records Managers: Mark McKinley, Christopher Lynch, Matilda Hagne, Daniel Kidane
Customer Service Manager: Louise McLaren
Senior Project Manager: Alan Pixsley
Project Managers: Cameron Kellow, Paulina Sapinska
Official Adjudicators: Ahmed Gamal Gabr, Anna Orford, Glenn Pollard, Jack Brockbank, Kimberley Dennis, Lena Kuhlmann, Lorenzo Veltri, Lucia Sinigagliesi, Paul Wiggins, Pete Fairbairn, Pravin Patel, Richard Stenning, Rishi Nath, Şeyda Subaşı-Gemici, Sofia Greenacre, Solvej Malouf, Swapnil Dangarikar

AMERICAS
SVP Americas: Peter Harper
VP Marketing & Commercial Sales: Keith Green
Director of Latin America: Carlos Martinez
Head of RMT – North America: Kimberly Partrick
Senior Account Managers: Nicole Pando, Ralph Hannah
Account Managers: Alex Angert, Lindsay Doran, Lisa Tobia, Giovanni Bruna, Mackenzie Berry
Project Manager: Casey DeSantis
PR Manager: Kristen Ott
Assistant PR Manager: Elizabeth Montoya
PR Co-ordinator: Sofia Rocher
Digital Co-ordinator: Kristen Stephenson
B2B Marketing Executive: Tavia Levy
Publishing Sales Manager: Lisa Corrado
Records Managers: Michael Furnari, Hannah Ortman, Kaitlin Holl, Raquel Assis, Sarah Casson
HR & Office Manager: Kellie Ferrick

Official Adjudicators: Christina Flounders Conlon, Evelyn Carrera, Jimmy Coggins, Michael Empric, Natalia Ramirez Talero, Carlos Tapia Rojas, Andrew Glass

JAPAN
VP Japan: Erika Ogawa
Office Manager: Fumiko Kitagawa
Director of RMT: Kaoru Ishikawa
Project Manager: Aya McMillan
Records Managers: Mariko Koike, Yoko Furuya
Designer: Momoko Cunneen
Senior PR Manager: Aya Tanaka
Senior PR & Sales Promotion Manager: Kazami Kamioka
Digital & Publishing Content Manager: Takafumi Suzuki
Commercial Director: Vihag Kulshrestha
Senior Marketing Executive: Asumi Funatsu
Account Manager: Takuro Maruyama
Senior Account Executive: Daisuke Katayama
Account Executive & Event Co-ordinator: Minami Ito
Official Adjudicators: Justin Patterson, Mai McMillan, Gulnaz Ukassova, Rei Iwashita

GREATER CHINA
President: Rowan Simons
General Manager: Madison Chang
Commercial Director: Blythe Fitzwiliam
Senior Account Manager: Catherine Gao, Lessi Li
Account Manager: Chloe Liu
Digital Business Manager: Jacky Yuan
Head of RMT: Charles Wharton
Records Manager: Alicia Zhao
External Relations Manager: Dong Cheng
Records Manager / Project Co-ordinator: Fay Jiang
HR & Office Manager: Tina Shi
Office Assistant: Kate Wang
Head of Marketing: Wendy Wang
B2B Marketing Manager: Iris Hou
Digital Manager: Lily Zeng
Marketing Executive: Tracy Cui
PR Manager: Ada Liu
Content Director: Angela Wu
Official Adjudicators: Joanne Brent, Brittany Dunn, John Garland, Maggie Luo

OFFICIALLY AMAZING

THE JIM PATTISON GROUP

GUINNESS WORLD RECORDS 2017

GUINNESS WORLD RECORDS™

BLOCK BUSTERS!

CONTENTS

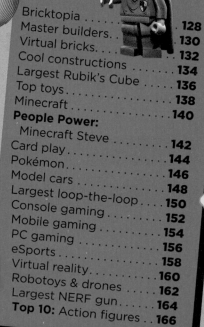

WELCOME TO BLOCKBUSTERS!

From Adele to *Zootopia*, *Guinness World Records 2017: Blockbusters!* is the ultimate almanac of the world's superlative movies, TV series, music, games and beyond. Discover which films rewrote box-office history, which books flew off the shelves and which online videos went viral in this go-to guide of smash hits.

Nowadays we enjoy pop culture in more forms than ever before, so this edition of *Blockbusters!* reflects that. The chapters are based on six of your favourite things to do: **Watch** (movies and TV), **Browse** (internet and social media), **Read** (books and magazines), **Play** (toys and games), **Go** (attractions and events) and **Consume** (shopping and brands).

As well as records for sales, awards and popularity, you'll also find special features on the real-life record-breakers that inspire the stories. For instance, find out which of Dory's sea-creature friends are record holders on pp.22–23. Meanwhile, *Star Trek* fans can go on a voyage of discovery to see out-of-this-world phenomena you might encounter on board the USS *Enterprise* (pp.42–43). We hope you enjoy the book!

Blockbusters! 2017 isn't just about records. It also packs in all your favourite features, including top 10s and stunning statistics, Q&As, quizzes and breathtaking photography. Here's a peek preview...

New chapters

Top 10s

Celebrity records

Awesome stats

Mini tables

Exclusive photos

Quick facts

Trending trivia

Exclusive Q&As

Extra info bars

Quizzes

Industry secrets

HOW TO BE A RECORD-BREAKER

You don't have to be Superman or Wonder Woman to set a record, although it *would* be an advantage! One of the best things about Guinness World Records is that *anyone* has the potential to become a record-breaker – including you! Below are a few of the key steps involved in the process...

1. Go to **www.guinnessworldrecords.com** and explore our records. New titles can also be suggested here.
2. Pick a record, click on "Apply Now" and request the guidelines. Ask us if you need any rules clarified.
3. Gather all the necessary equipment and plan out the logistics, such as witnesses and venues, etc.
4. Practise, practise, practise!
5. Before you attempt the record, check off all the guidelines. Make sure that all requested data is captured (e.g., video, photos, statements).
6. Upload your evidence and await the result.
7. If successful, put your certificate in pride of place and show it off at every opportunity! If not, don't give up. Apply again or pick a different record.

GWR GETS OUT AND ABOUT...

To keep our finger firmly on the pop-culture pulse, this year the *Blockbusters!* team has mostly been racing BB-8 robots, watching "Chewbacca Mom" laugh on loop and playing endless hours of *Pokémon Go*. All in the interests of research, of course...

As you'll see in the photos below, we've attended some of 2016's hottest events too, such as conventions, videogame launches and movie premieres. They've offered us the chance to catch up with record-breakers – old and new – and present the stars with their official GWR certificates. These events are also the perfect opportunity to get the inside track on the potential blockbusters of the future.

FINDING DORY

LONDON COMIC CON

LEGO® STAR WARS: THE FORCE AWAKENS

CALLING ALL MASTER BUILDERS

TRANSFORM INTO CAPTAIN PANTASTIC!

SET YOUR OWN BLOCKBUSTER RECORD NOW!

As you read this book, keep an eye out for golden rosettes. They indicate that there's a related record you can try at home. All of these records are making their debut in *Blockbusters! 2017*, so be one of the first to try them out! Head to pp.208–09 for details. Of course, you're welcome to attempt any of the records you read about, though it's best to ask a grown-up for help getting started; see opposite for more on the GWR application process.

GET FACE-TO-FACE WITH EMOJI

TAKE ON A TEAM TOY CHALLENGE

DO I KNOW YOU?

Dory is renowned for her forgetfulness, but the notion that fishes have a "three-second memory" is actually a myth. Studies have found that fish can recall things for several months.

WATCH

CAPTAIN AMERICA
& THE AVENGERS

Star-spangled super-soldier Steve Rogers has been protecting the world from the forces of evil since the 1940s. The Captain, who was very nearly called "Super American", got his big movie reboot with 2011's *The First Avenger*. His latest outing is *Civil War* (main picture), in which he is pitted against his Avenger allies. This marks his third leading role in the Marvel movie universe.

HIGHEST-GROSSING SUPERHERO MOVIE

Superheroes have taken the big screen by storm in the last few years, but none drew more people to movie theatres than Marvel's *The Avengers* (2012). The film, featuring Captain America, Iron Man, Black Widow and gang, Hulk-smashed all the comic-book competition by taking $1,511,757,910 (£938.4 m) at the worldwide box office during its 22 weeks on release.

$2.22 bn
Combined global takings for the three *Captain America* movies – half of which was earned by the third release, *Civil War*, in 2016.

The Avengers' employer SHIELD has stood for different things over its history; today it means Strategic Homeland Intervention, Enforcement and Logistics Division.

HEAVY METAL
HOW DOES CAPTAIN AMERICA'S SHIELD STAND UP TO OTHER MARVEL-LOUS WEAPONS?

	CAPTAIN AMERICA	THOR	WOLVERINE
Weapon	Shield	Hammer (aka Mjölnir)	Claws
Metal	Vibranium & iron	Uru	Adamantium (iron alloy)
Source	Meteorite & Earth	Asgard	Earth
Properties	Absorbs kinetic energy	Returns to owner; summons lightning; opens portals	Indestructible (virtually); razor-sharp; very expensive

DID YOU KNOW?

Captain America is one of a select few superheroes to have been deemed "worthy" (or at least powerful) enough to lift Thor's hammer, Mjölnir. Others include Magneto, Wonder Woman and Thunderstrike.

MOST OFFICIAL SUPERHERO COSTUMES IN A VIDEOGAME

As of 29 Feb 2016, US developer Gazillion Entertainment had released 404 superhero costumes for its superhero MMORPG *Marvel Heroes 2016*, with each outfit officially adapted from either a comic book or movie. This included 23 outfits for Iron Man, 19 for Spider-Man (example left) and a respectable 15 for the Captain (example right).

MOST PROFITABLE ACTOR

For every $1 (£0.65) paid to Marvel's Captain America, Chris Evans (USA), his movies grossed $181.80 (£118). According to Forbes, Evans – whose blockbusters include *Captain America: The Winter Soldier* (2014) and *Avengers: Age of Ultron* (2015) – returned more profit relative to his pay than any other Hollywood actor.

KUNG FU PANDA

Po the panda defied all the odds to become a kung fu master in his debut movie in 2008. With the 2016 release of his third film, we celebrate the real-life record-breakers that make up the Furious Five and the Dragon Warrior.

LARGEST WILD CAT

Male Siberian, or Amur, tigers (*Panthera tigris altaica*) can reach 3.3 m (10 ft 9 in) from nose to tail. Females, such as Master Tigress, tend to be a little smaller at 2.7 m (8 ft 10 in) long but are no less fearsome!

NEWEST SNUB-NOSED MONKEY

Trickster-turned-hero Monkey is a golden snub-nosed monkey (*Rhinopithecus roxellana*) from China. The related Myanmar snub-nosed monkey (*R. strykeri*, above) was found in Burma as recently as 2010.

HUNGRIEST BEAR

Po is known to be partial to a dumpling or two. While any self-respecting real panda would probably turn their nose up at dumplings, Po's ample appetite is typical of these hungry bears. Each day, giant pandas (*Ailuropoda melanoleuca*) eat as much as 38% of their own weight in bamboo shoots. That equates to an eight-year-old child chowing down on about 189 Mars bars!

TALLEST FLYING BIRD

In the *Kung Fu Panda* movies, Master Crane stands head and shoulders above his friends... In fact, he and his relatives – belonging to the Gruidae family – are the tallest of any birds to take to the air, with some members standing 2 m (6 ft 6 in) off the ground!

LARGEST MANTIS

The Furious Five's smallest fighter, Mantis, once said, "Fear the bug!" If bigger equals scarier, then the 20-cm-long (7.8-in) flower mantis *Toxodera denticulata* from Java, Indonesia, is the most monstrous mantis. But beware: there are reports of even bigger mantises lurking in South American rainforests...

MOST VENOMOUS VIPER

Master Viper may not have any fangs, but her kung fu skills mean she isn't any less deadly. Her real-life cousin, the saw-scaled viper (*Echis carinatus*, above), meanwhile, prefers more traditional methods. One bite from this serpent can deliver as much as 12 mg of venom; just half of that is enough to kill an adult human.

LARGEST MARTIAL ARTS DISPLAY

Of course, humans love kung fu as much as the next animated panda... In 2009, a total of 33,996 people were gathered by the Beijing Municipal Bureau of Sports to perform martial arts outside the Bird's Nest stadium in the Chinese capital. The event was part of the country's very first national fitness day.

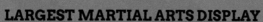

STAR WARS

The Force is strong with this one... As of Feb 2016, the seven *Star Wars* movies released had earned in excess of $6.45 bn (£4.5 bn) globally, easily making it the highest-grossing sci-fi film series in the galaxy.

BIGGEST MOVIE PREMIERE IN HOLLYWOOD

On 14 Dec 2015, the Los Angeles premiere of *The Force Awakens* took place across a quarter-mile stretch of Hollywood Boulevard. The film screened in three venues – the TCL Chinese Theatre, the Dolby Theatre and El Capitan – with a total capacity of 6,700 seats.

CONFIDENTIAL

RUMOUR HAS IT...

Set to hit theatres in 2018 is a new *Star Wars* movie reported to explore Han Solo's backstory. This is one of three projected spin-offs based in the wider *SW* universe. The first, *Rogue One*, is due out in Dec 2016, while a further episode focusing on Boba Fett is scheduled for 2020.

FASTEST MOVIE TO GROSS $1 BILLION

The long-anticipated seventh instalment in the *Star Wars* saga, *The Force Awakens*, rewrote box-office history. Among the many records it smashed was the quickest time to reach $1 bn in ticket sales. It achieved the feat in just 12 days, beating the 13 days set by *Jurassic World* (2015).

30.65
Millions who watched the second teaser of *The Force Awakens* uploaded to YouTube on 16 Apr 2015. It is the most viewed movie trailer in 24 hr.

WOW!

Q&A WITH... CHLOE BRUCE

The stunt double for Daisy Ridley (Rey) in *SW Episode VII* is a Force to be reckoned with...

Q How did you break into the stunt industry?

A I first got into the stunt industry by auditioning to be a part of Disney's *John Carter* [2012]. I was used as a special action extra in that, and then from there I was fortunate enough to meet many people in the industry and next was asked to join the stunt team on *Wrath of the Titans* [2012].

Q What was it like working with Daisy Ridley?

A Working alongside Daisy [below] on *The Force Awakens* was incredible. She is such a determined and lovely girl.

We actually get along really well. She trains super-hard and wants to do as much of the action as she can. She was a dream to work with.

Q If you had Jedi powers in real life, how would you use them?

A I guess I would use them in more practical ways. If I couldn't carry something by myself, I could lift it or move it using the Force. I could use my powers to enhance my reactions within everyday life. I could also use Jedi mind tricks to my advantage to help the law – maybe to ensure that people are being honest.

Q A lot of your movies are based on comic books, e.g. *Guardians of the Galaxy* (below) and *Thor 2*. Is this a favourite genre?

A I love watching these kind of action movies, but I think this is also because I am normally either involved with them, or I know the stunt teams that worked on them. In fact, my favourite movies are based on real-life events.

WHAT A TROOPER!

Ashley Broomhall (UK) climbed England's highest peak – the 978-m (3,209-ft) Scafell Pike in Lake District National Park, Cumbria, UK – in May 2016. He was kitted out in rather unconventional hiking gear: a Stormtrooper outfit! He had already scaled Snowdon in Wales and Ben Nevis in Scotland the year before. Across the three peaks, that makes for a total height of 3,408 m (11,181 ft) climbed. Broomhall took on the challenge to raise money for the charity Cancer Research UK. Not surprisingly, Broomhall is a member of the 501st Legion – the **largest *Star Wars* costuming group**, with 8,122 members.

STAR WARS

The Star Wars galaxy extends far, far beyond movie theatres. The epic story and memorable characters have inspired videogames, apps, books, TV series, toys, clothes and even hairstyles. So it's not only the films that are setting records...

MOST EXPENSIVE FIGURINES SOLD AT AUCTION

A collection of Action Man and Star Wars figurines, still in their packaging, sold for a record £180,000 ($277,546) at Vectis Auctions, UK, on 27 May 2015. The lot, which also included action figure costumes, vehicles and other accessories, was sold by retired toy salesman Doug Carpenter, who had been storing them in his garage since the 1980s.

MOST ARCADE GAMES BASED ON A FILM LICENCE

As of Sep 2016, there had been eight official arcade machines inspired by the *Star Wars* saga. The most recent was Bandai Namco's *Star Wars: Battle Pod* (2015), released as a standard cabinet and also as two "premium editions" (example above; see fact opposite).

LARGEST RANGE OF STAR WARS TOYS-TO-LIFE FIGURES

A total of 19 *Star Wars* characters were released for *Disney Infinity 3.0* (2015), the last title in the toys-to-life series. Figures come from various movies and spin-offs, and include Yoda, Ahsoka Tano and Darth Vader, plus Finn and Rey from *The Force Awakens*.

MOST VALUABLE CARD IN *STAR WARS: CARD TRADER*

Star Wars: Card Trader is a mobile app that lets fans collect and exchange digital cards based on the *Star Wars* universe. The rarest of these is the Vintage "Han in the Millennium Falcon", of which only 1,500 are available. Copies have sold online for as much as $224.99 (£151.75).

So what makes the record-breaking *Battle Pod* (opposite) so "premium"? Its features include moving leather seats, an engraved plaque and even your name in the credits!

MOST VALUABLE MOVIE FRANCHISE

According to *Fortune* magazine, the Star Wars empire was worth approximately $41.98 bn (£29.46 bn) as of 31 Jan 2016 – more than any other film franchise. Of this, the box-office take from the seven theatrical releases in the main series accounted for about a fifth of the total. Home video and digital sales of the movies brought in $5.75 bn (£4 bn), toys and merchandise sales (left) were estimated at $17 bn (£11.9 bn), and a further $4.28 bn (£3 bn) was attributed to videogames. The first of these three spin-off movies, *Rogue One* (2016, below and inset), will no doubt add yet another sizeable chunk of profit in both box-office and merchandise sales.

PIXAR PERFECT

Pixar has been pushing the boundaries of animated cinema since *Toy Story* revolutionized the movie industry back in 1995. With the 2016 release of *Finding Dory*, the studio has now produced 17 feature-length films, with sequels like *Cars 3* and *The Incredibles 2* already in the works.

TOP 5 PIXAR MOVIES

Toy Story 3 (2010)	$1.06 bn (£678.5 m)
Finding Nemo (2003)	$936.4 m (£583.2 m)
Finding Dory (2016)	$915.6 m (£699.4 m)
Inside Out (2015)	$853.9 m (£652.3 m)
Monsters University (2013, left)	$743.5 m (£454.2 m)

Source: The-Numbers.com; correct as of 23 Aug 2016

LARGEST OBJECT LIFTED BY BALLOONS

Taking inspiration from one of the most iconic scenes in the heartwarming movie *Up* (2009), the Nat Geo Channel (USA) sent a building soaring using 300 helium balloons. The "hover-house", which weighed 4,335 lb (1,966.3 kg), reached 1.8 mi (3 km) above Los Angeles, California, USA, in 2011.

The hopping lamp that appears in Pixar's logo and intro sequences is called Luxo Jr. It comes from the studio's very first animated short movie, made in 1986.

HIGHEST-GROSSING UNDERWATER MOVIE

No other film set in the ocean has hauled in more at the box office than *Finding Nemo* (2003), with takings of $936,429,370 (£583.2 m) as of 23 Aug 2016. Pixar *fin*-atics can check out pp.20–23 for more on the hit *sea*-quel, *Finding Dory*.

FIRST ANIMATED MOVIE TO GROSS $1 BILLION

Long before *Frozen* (2013) came along and rewrote box-office history, Pixar was truly breaking new ground in cinema. Not only was the original *Toy Story* (1995, below) the **first feature-length computer-animated movie**, but 2010's third instalment was the first to surpass $1 bn (£681 m).

CONFIDENTIAL

RUMOUR HAS IT...

After what would be a hiatus of eight years, *Toy Story 4* is due to be released in 2018 – so get ready to go to infinity and beyond once more!

HIGHEST AVERAGE GROSS FOR A MOVIE STUDIO

With many blockbusters under its belt, including *The Incredibles* (2004), *Ratatouille* (2007) and *Inside Out* (2015, main picture), Pixar is king based on its income-to-movie ratio. Having earned $10,650,908,391 (£7.98 bn) worldwide from 17 feature films since 1995, Pixar has averaged $626,524,023 (£469.9 m) per title as of 4 Aug 2016. Check out its biggest hits in the table opposite.

FINDING DORY

With the huge success of *Finding Nemo* in 2003, it was only a matter of time before the much-loved characters made waves with a sequel. After a 13-year interlude, *Finding Dory* arrived in 2016.

HIGHEST-GROSSING DAY FOR AN ANIMATED MOVIE

Three-and-a-half years in the making, *Finding Dory* made a big splash, earning $54,746,405 (£38.6 m) on its first day of release in the USA (17 Jun 2016), according to The-Numbers.com. The same weekend, it also became the **fastest animated movie to gross $100 million**, taking just two days to surpass the milestone.

9
Versions of *Finding Dory* screened to Pixar's Braintrust before the final cut. The internal group of Pixar employees reviews all the studio's movies before release.

FINDING DORY QUIZ
FORGET DORY, HOW GOOD IS *YOUR* MEMORY?

1. What was the title of the short film that aired before *Finding Dory*?

2. What is the name of the third sea lion who tries to climb on the rock?

3. In what colour bucket does Becky carry Marlin and Nemo?

(Answers right)

The Marine Life Institute in *Finding Dory* is largely based on California's Monterey Bay Aquarium. Pixar made many research trips there during the making of the film.

WHERE WAS THE TANK GANG?

In a post-credits sequence, we briefly see the "Tank Gang" from *Finding Nemo*. Co-director Andrew Stanton revealed that the Tank Gang once had a much larger part, playing a *"Mission: Impossible* team that helped Marlin and Nemo find Dory". To keep the focus on Dory, however, they were chopped. "It was a hard thing to cut," Stanton admitted, "but the second we did it... everything improved 100%."

THE STORY OF DORY

At the UK premiere of *Finding Dory* on 10 Jul 2016, Guinness World Records presented the film-makers with their certificates. On the challenges of writing a movie in which the main character suffers from short-term memory loss, Andrew Stanton (above right) said: "It took the most intelligent crew I've ever had. It brought us to our knees many times. There's a grocery list of tricks we learned that are all in the film now to keep you invested [in Dory], even though she can't remember a lot!"

MOST FOLLOWERS ON TWITTER FOR A TV PERSONALITY

Absent-minded Dory probably wouldn't be very good at keeping her social media up to date. But Ellen DeGeneres (USA, left), who voices her, is a high-ranking member of the Twitterati. As of 5 Sep 2016, she had 61,848,366 followers.

ANSWERS: 1. Piper 2. Gerald 3. Green

FINDING DORY

In honour of *Finding Dory*, join us on an ocean odyssey as we celebrate a few fishy records inspired by the movie's characters.

LARGEST RAY

Teacher Mr Ray (below) is a spotted eagle ray (*Aetobatus narinari*), which in real life measure up to 3 m (9 ft 10.1 in) across. Much bigger is its relative the Atlantic manta ray (*Manta birostris*, right), with an average wing-span of 5.2–6.8 m (17–22 ft 3 in)!

LARGEST OCTOPUS

"Septopus" Hank is probably the crankiest of the new characters. This is a pretty fair reflection of his kind, as the vast majority of octopuses live alone. Ruby octopuses, like Hank, are often mistaken for the similar-looking *Enteroctopus dofleini*, or Pacific giant octopus (above). These truly are sea monsters, with the largest on record boasting an arm-span of 9.6 m (31 ft 6 in).

DID YOU KNOW?

Dory is a Pacific royal blue tang (*Paracanthurus hepatus*), a species found in reefs throughout the Pacific and Indian Oceans. A member of the surgeonfish family, these fish play a vital role in helping coral to survive by keeping algae in check.

The leatherback turtle holds the distinction of being the **deepest-diving chelonian**. One fitted with a recording device reached a depth of 1,200 m (3,937 ft) in 1987.

NO STING IN THE TALE

Why can Marlin and Nemo make their home in a sea anemone that stings every other creature? It comes down to an extra-thick coat of mucus on their skin. Some clownfish are born with full protection, while others need a period of acclimatization. In return, they supply anemones with nutrients, as well as keeping parasites and predators at bay.

FASTEST TURTLE

Crush (right) is about as chilled out as they come, but a Pacific leatherback turtle (*Dermochelys coriacea*, inset) was once clocked at 35 km/h (22 mph). That makes it the speediest marine reptile ever.

LARGEST FISH

Dory's "pipe pal" Destiny is the ultimate giant of the fish world: the aptly named whale shark (*Rhincodon typus*). The average length for a whale shark is 8 m (26 ft 2 in) – double the size of a great white shark! The largest ever recorded was a staggering 12.65 m (41 ft 6 in). Despite its mega-mouth, which gapes 1.5 m (4 ft 11 in) wide on average, this fish filter-feeds on tiny plankton, such as eggs and larvae.

X-MEN

Everyone's favourite mutants joined forces again in 2016 to battle a vengeful ancient god in *X-Men: Apocalypse* (below), boosting the main series' total takings to $2.79 bn (£2.13 bn).

$577,036,449
Average gross of the movies in which comic-book writer Stan Lee has made a cameo appearance. His most successful to date is *The Avengers* (2012), in which he played himself.

WOW

HIGHEST-GROSSING ACTOR FROM CAMEO APPEARANCES ONLY

With movies based on his work frequently breaking records, it's not surprising that Marvel mastermind Stan Lee (USA) would want to play a part in the action. Since making his screen debut in the non-Marvel indie film *Mallrats* (1995), Lee has appeared in 30 releases – including *Ant-Man* (2015), *Captain America: Civil War* (2016) and, most recently, *X-Men: Apocalypse* (right). Combined, his films had grossed $17,311,093,469 (£13 bn) as of 2 Aug 2016.

MOST EXPENSIVE *X-MEN* COMIC

The highest price ever realized by an *X-Men* comic is $492,937.50 (£318,014). The sum was paid for a copy of issue #1 (1963, right), which was sold by Heritage Auctions (USA) on 26 Jul 2012.

LARGEST COLLECTION OF X-MEN MEMORABILIA

Eric Jaskolka (USA) started reading *X-Men* comic books in 1989, sparking a life-long passion. By 2012, he had collected 15,400 items, including more than 6,000 comics, 3,500 trading cards and hundreds of figurines.

TOP 5 X-MEN MOVIES

Days of Future Past (2014, top right)	$747,862,775 (£462.3 m)
Apocalypse (2016)	$530,842,489 (£401.6 m)
The Last Stand (2006)	$459,359,555 (£242.4 m)
The Wolverine (2013)	$416,456,852 (£254.2 m)
Origins: Wolverine (2009, bottom right)	$374,825,760 (£230.9 m)

Source: The-Numbers.com; correct as of 2 Aug 2016

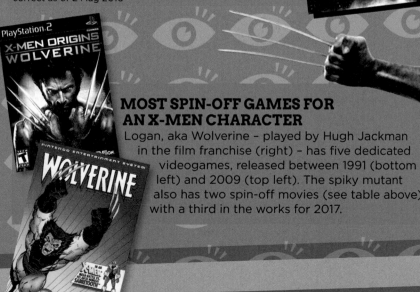

MOST SPIN-OFF GAMES FOR AN X-MEN CHARACTER

Logan, aka Wolverine – played by Hugh Jackman in the film franchise (right) – has five dedicated videogames, released between 1991 (bottom left) and 2009 (top left). The spiky mutant also has two spin-off movies (see table above), with a third in the works for 2017.

PEOPLE POWER: GHOSTBUSTERS

LARGEST GATHERING OF PEOPLE DRESSED AS GHOSTS
The red-carpet event held to mark the Southeast Asia release of the 2016 *Ghostbusters* movie was haunted by a *spook*-tacular 263 phantoms, each tagged with the iconic "no ghosts" logo. Director Paul Feig and star Melissa McCarthy (inset) mingled with the restless spirits at the Marina Bay Sands Expo & Convention Centre in Singapore on 12 Jun 2016.

Everyone's favourite green ghoul, Slimer, was originally called Onion Head because of his nasty stink. He gained his new identity in spin-off cartoon *The Real Ghostbusters*.

$508,218,523

Total box-office takings for the original *Ghostbusters* movies, released in 1984 and 1989. For eight weeks, the first film held the title of most watched movie.

I AIN'T AFRAID OF NO TROLLS

Who you gonna call? Maybe *not* the new Ghostbusters team. The trailer for the paranormal reboot had received 1,000,877 dislikes on YouTube by 16 Aug 2016 – the **most disliked movie trailer**. Happily, however, the film went on to take a respectable $226,628,697 (£171.6 m) by 15 Sep 2016.

THE REAL SECRET LIVES OF PETS

Max, Snowball, Ozone and the gang have nothing on these amazing animals, who have mastered some impressive tricks to earn their records...

THE DOG THAT LIKES TO ROLL

Norman the Briard, owned by Karen Cobb (USA), has some pretty unusual ways of getting from A to B. Not only did he achieve the **fastest 30 m on a scooter by a dog** (20.77 sec), but he also holds the record for the **fastest 30 m on a bicycle by a dog** (55.41 sec; inset right).

WOW!

1,085 hr 26 min
Estimated time it would take Norman to complete the Tour de France cycling race at his record pace. That's just over 45 days!

THE ANIMATED ANIMALS THAT BREAK RECORDS

Universal Pictures' *The Secret Life of Pets* (left) opened at 4,370 US cinemas on 8 Jul 2016, making it the **widest release for an animated movie**. It went on to gross $104,352,905 (£72 m) in just three days, which is the **highest-grossing opening weekend for an original movie** (i.e., not based on pre-existing characters or stories), beating 2015's *Inside Out*.

THE CAT THAT CAN MULTI-TASK

Super-talented Didga performed the **most tricks by a cat in one minute** – 24 – with her owner Robert Dollwet (USA/AUS) in Tweed Heads, New South Wales, Australia, on 5 Feb 2016. Tricks included jumping (left), high-fiving (below), spinning, rolling over and riding a skateboard.

THE FISH THAT PLAYS SOCCER

Scoring goals is just one of Einstein the goldfish's talents. Guided by his owner, Dean Pomerleau (USA), he demonstrated a total of six skills in 2005 – the **largest repertoire of tricks for a fish**.

THE (GUINEA) PIG THAT FLIES

On 6 Apr 2012, Truffles cleared 48 cm (18.8 in) in Rosyth, Fife, UK, to achieve the **longest jump by a guinea pig**. This beat his own record for the second time, with his previous leaps spanning 30 cm (11.8 in) and 40 cm (15.7 in).

THE PARROT THAT SHOOTS HOOPS

The **most slam-dunks by a parrot in one minute** is 22, set by Zac the macaw in San Jose, California, USA, on 30 Dec 2011. Trained by Julie and Ed Cardoza (USA), Zac can also roll over, ride a bike and raise a flag, among other tricks (also see pp.198–99).

BATMAN V SUPERMAN

BLOCKBUSTER CHALLENGE
See pp.208–09

Some of DC Comics' most iconic caped crusaders, including Superman, Batman and Wonder Woman (pictured), united forces in 2016 blockbuster *Batman v Superman: Dawn of Justice*. It grossed a punchy $852,018,506 (£585.8 m) globally.

56

Number of baddies in *LEGO Batman 3: Beyond Gotham* (TT Games, 2014) – the most villains in a Batman videogame.

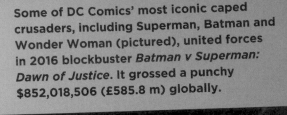

LARGEST COLLECTION OF BATMAN MEMORABILIA

With almost half a century of collecting under his utility belt, Kevin Silva (USA) boasted 2,501 pieces of Batman merchandise as of 25 Oct 2013. It all started with a lunchbox given to him as a child.

TOP 5 BATMAN MOVIES

The Dark Knight Rises (2012)	$1.08 bn (£672.4 m)	
The Dark Knight (2008)	$1.00 bn (£505 m)	
Batman (1989)	$411.3 m (£259.6 m)	
Batman Begins (2005)	$359.1 m (£201.3 m)	
Batman Forever (1995)	$336.5 m (£213.1 m)	
Source: The-Numbers.com; correct as of 6 Sep 2016		

LARGEST GATHERING OF PEOPLE DRESSED AS BATMAN

When Canadian company Nexen Energy sent out the "Bat" signal, 542 workers answered on 18 Sep 2014. As per the GWR guidelines, each participant had to dress in a complete Batman costume. This included a full body outfit, cape, utility belt, black boots and face mask with bat ears.

Batman and Superman first met in 1952 on a cruise ship in issue #76 of the *Superman* comic. The superheroes teamed up to catch a diamond thief.

LARGEST GATHERING OF PEOPLE DRESSED AS SUPERMAN

When it comes to the battle of the lookalikes, Metropolis's hero beats his Gotham rival. Fancy-dress specialist Escapade (UK) assembled 867 super-people in Lowther, Cumbria, UK, on 27 Jul 2013. That's a lot of spandex!

MOST EXPENSIVE COMIC

Action Comics #1 from 1938 – with Superman showing off his strength on the cover – sold for $3,207,852 (£2 m) to Metropolis Collectibles (USA) at an online auction on 24 Aug 2014. Another copy of the same issue sold for $956,000 (£728,000) in 2016.

$130
Amount paid by DC Comics for the rights to Superman in 1938; ironically, the cheque for the purchase sold for $160,000 in 2012!

TOP 5 SUPERMAN MOVIES

Man of Steel (2013)	$667.9 m (£418.6 m)
Superman Returns (2006)	$374 m (£196 m)
Superman (1978)	$300.2 m (£148.6 m)
Superman II (1980)	$108.1 m (£58.8 m)
Superman III (1983)	$59.9 m (£40.4 m)

Source: The-Numbers.com; correct as of 6 Sep 2016

THE BIG PICTURE

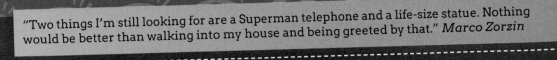
"Two things I'm still looking for are a Superman telephone and a life-size statue. Nothing would be better than walking into my house and being greeted by that." *Marco Zorzin*

Brazilian super-collector Marco Superman Zorzin (yes, his middle name really *is* Superman!) owned 1,518 items of Man of Steel merchandise – the **largest collection of Superman memorabilia** – as verified on 14 Feb 2016. Explaining how it began, Marco said: "I have always been a fan. As young as three or four, I have memories of sitting with my dad watching the movies and waiting for him to appear. The first items I bought were three Eaglemoss Superman statues and, after that, I never really stopped."

THE ALIENS ARE COMING!

They come in many forms, sizes and colours, and you never know if they want to hug you or zap you, but no matter their motives, aliens have been entertaining us at the cinema for decades.

1:12
Scale of the White House model that was used in the iconic scene from *Independence Day* (pictured). It took 40 explosive charges to destroy it.

HIGHEST-GROSSING ALIEN-INVASION MOVIE

The original *Independence Day* (above) grossed $817 m (£530 m), making it the most profitable film of 1996. Two decades later, its highly anticipated sequel, *Independence Day: Resurgence* (right), landed at cinemas. But it didn't quite live up to its predecessor, having taken $386,237,295 (£290.6 m) by 13 Sep 2016, according to The-Numbers.com.

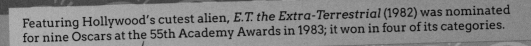

Featuring Hollywood's cutest alien, *E.T. the Extra-Terrestrial* (1982) was nominated for nine Oscars at the 55th Academy Awards in 1983; it won in four of its categories.

FIRST ANIMATED FEATURE PRODUCED IN STEREOSCOPIC 3D

Until 2009, animated movies were converted to 3D *after* they were completed. *Monsters vs. Aliens*, however, was rendered in true stereoscopic 3D from the beginning, an expensive process that added $15 m (£9.4 m) to the budget.

SLOWEST CLOUDS

No, it's not a flying saucer – it's a lenticular cloud. They form in still pockets of air created by the movement of the wind over hills and mountains. Unlike other clouds, they barely move at all, even when there are strong winds on the ground. Their odd shape and dense appearance often mean that they are mistaken for mysterious aircraft.

FIRST SCIENTIFIC INVESTIGATION INTO FOIL HATS

People who believe that aliens (or a secret government organization) are controlling their minds have often relied on aluminium headgear for protection. In 2005, students at the Massachusetts Institute of Technology, USA, decided to put this conspiracy-theorist home remedy to the test. Interestingly, the results suggested that foil hats can actually *amplify* radio signals at some frequencies, particularly those controlled by the US government.

LARGEST COLLECTION OF ALIENS

Lisa Vanderperre-Hirsch of Florida, USA, shares her home with a total of 547 grey alien-related items, including figurines, masks and even extraterrestrial toilet paper. In 2014, Lisa was selected as a finalist in the crew selection process for the Mars One space mission – so one day she could become a real-life Martian!

LITTLE GREEN MEN

The *Toy Story* aliens teleported to the 2016 Academy Awards to join co-stars Woody and Buzz Lightyear. They were there to celebrate 20 years since their debut and also to present the Oscar for Best Animated Film to fellow Pixar release *Inside Out* (2015).

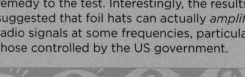

ICE AGE

Since their first appearance in 2002, Manny, Sid, Diego and Scrat have faced everything from mega floods to dinosaurs. Their latest adventure, *Collision Course*, pitted the gang against their biggest enemy yet – planet-smashing asteroids!

ONE SMALL STEP. ONE GIANT MESS.

ICE AGE
COLLISION COURSE

LARGEST MAMMOTH

Manny's biggest relative was the Steppe mammoth (*Mammuthus trogontherii*), which roamed over central Europe a million years ago. This hairy cousin of modern elephants stood around 4.5 m (14 ft 9 in) tall at the shoulder.

LARGEST SLOTH

Sid is a ground sloth, a relative of today's sloths that live in trees. He's actually pretty small for his kind, though. The largest ground sloth, the extinct *Eremotherium eomigrans* (right), reached 5.2 m (17 ft) high on its hind legs!

ICE AGE MOVIES

TITLE	GROSS
Continental Drift (2012)	$879.7 m (£561.8 m)
Dawn of the Dinosaurs (2009)	$859.7 m (£515.4 m)
The Meltdown (2006)	$651.8 m (£342 m)
Ice Age (2002)	$386.1 m (£249.2 m)
Collision Course (2016)	$314.9 m (£240.5 m)

Source: The-Numbers.com; correct as of 23 Aug 2016

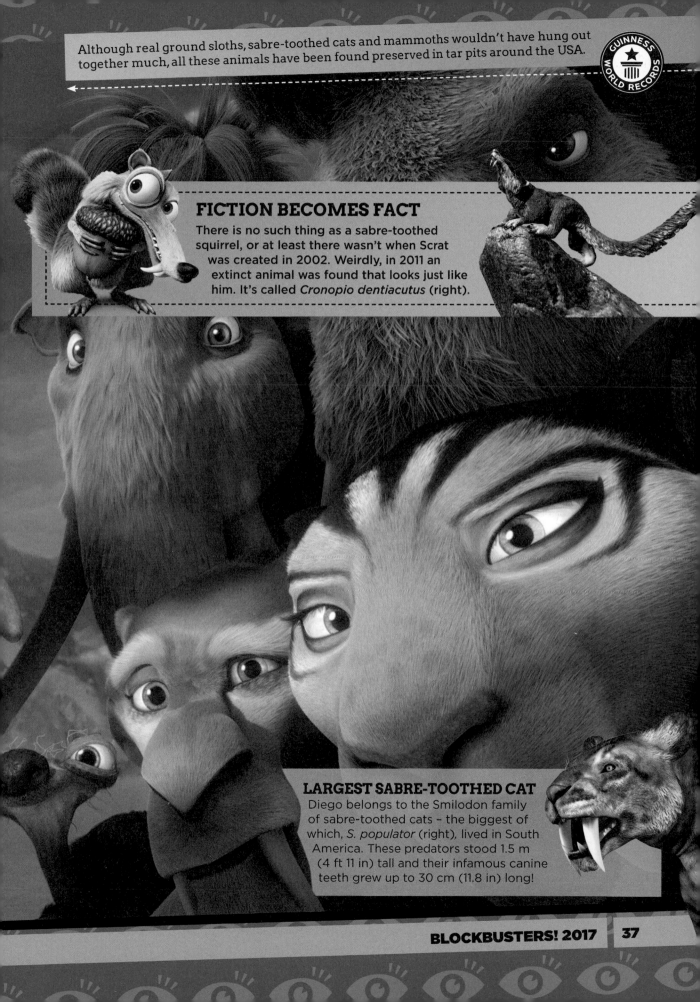

Although real ground sloths, sabre-toothed cats and mammoths wouldn't have hung out together much, all these animals have been found preserved in tar pits around the USA.

FICTION BECOMES FACT

There is no such thing as a sabre-toothed squirrel, or at least there wasn't when Scrat was created in 2002. Weirdly, in 2011 an extinct animal was found that looks just like him. It's called *Cronopio dentiacutus* (right).

LARGEST SABRE-TOOTHED CAT

Diego belongs to the Smilodon family of sabre-toothed cats – the biggest of which, *S. populator* (right), lived in South America. These predators stood 1.5 m (4 ft 11 in) tall and their infamous canine teeth grew up to 30 cm (11.8 in) long!

GAMES TO MOVIES

Whether it's epic tales played out on consoles or addictive mini-adventure phone apps, movie-makers are catching on that much-loved stories and characters from the "game-iverse" work just as well on the big screen.

HIGHEST-GROSSING VIDEOGAME MOVIE ADAPTATION

No other film inspired by a videogame has earned more at the box office than 2016's *Warcraft*. Based on the famous battle MMO, the movie takes viewers behind enemy lines to reveal the stories of both the humans and the orcs. By 9 Aug 2016, it had made $433,125,655 (£331.5 m).

HIGHEST-GROSSING ANIMATED MOVIE BASED ON A VIDEOGAME

In 2013, *Angry Birds* became the **first app to sell movie rights**. The film of the same name, starring bushy-browed Red (main picture), slingshotted itself to this box-office record, having earned $346,634,366 (£265.3 m) worldwide by 9 Aug 2016. It is the second-highest-grossing videogame adaptation, beaten only by *Warcraft* (above).

MORE GAMES TO MOVIES

RATCHET & CLANK

In 2016, we discovered how the Lombax and robot duo met and joined forces to defeat the evil Blarg.

ASSASSIN'S CREED

Michael Fassbender played two characters in this 2016 time-hopping adventure.

To celebrate the release of *Star Fox Zero* in 2016, Fox McCloud got an animated short, *The Battle Begins*.

FIRST LIVE-ACTION MOVIE BASED ON A VIDEOGAME

Released in 1993, the trailblazing *Super Mario Bros.* cast Bob Hoskins (above right) and John Leguizamo as the world's favourite moustachioed plumbers. There have been rumours that Nintendo and Sony were in talks about a new movie, so Mario and Luigi may make a big-screen comeback soon.

MOST MOVIE SPIN-OFFS FROM A VIDEOGAME SERIES

Pokémon has inspired no fewer than 19 feature-length movies to date. The debut, *Pokémon: The First Movie* (1998), was the most successful, taking $163,644,662 (£102.2 m) globally. The latest instalment was 2015's *Hoopa and the Clash of Ages* (above). Off the back of *Pokémon Go*'s success in 2016, a live-action film, centred on a character called Detective Pikachu, will start production in 2017.

SONIC THE HEDGEHOG

Announced in Feb 2016 – the year of Sonic's 25th birthday – Sega's flagship spiky speedster is due to get his very first movie by 2018. Like *Warcraft*, there are plans for it to be part live-action and part animation.

STAR TREK

It's been more than 50 years since the original series made its TV debut in 1966, but the *Star Trek* universe is still expanding. The latest film, *Star Trek Beyond* (below), opened to glowing reviews in Jul 2016 and a new TV show, *Star Trek: Discovery,* is due to air in early 2017.

$59.25 m
Earned by *Star Trek Beyond* in its opening weekend, seeing off competition from *Ice Age: Collision Course.* It falls a little short of the two other *Star Trek* reboots, though.

HIGHEST-GROSSING *STAR TREK* MOVIE

Of the 13 *Star Trek* movies to have boldly gone to the cinema to date, none has been more successful than *Star Trek Into Darkness* (right), which grossed $467,381,584 (£296.4 m) in 2013. This also makes it the **most successful sci-fi television adaptation**. The third entry in the rebooted series, *Star Trek Beyond* (above), hit screens in Jul 2016. It had earned a respectable $285,393,322 (£214.5 m) by 5 Sep 2016, according to The-Numbers.com.

LARGEST STAR TREK MAZE

This next record is officially a–*maze*-ing! Each year, Tom Pearcy (UK) creates a brand-new maze out of, well, maize in York, UK. His themed labyrinths have been inspired by everything from *Harry Potter* to *Doctor Who*. In 2006, *Star Trek* was chosen to celebrate the original TV show's 40th anniversary. The design included a Star Fleet badge and the *Enterprise* battling with a Borg cube, over an area of 18 acres (7.2 hectares).

The theme of the maze in 2016 was Roald Dahl characters, such as Willy Wonka and the BFG, in honour of the author's centenary (see pp.114–15).

SMALLEST STARSHIP *ENTERPRISE*

Takayuki Hoshino and Shinji Matsui of the Himeji Institute of Technology in Japan used an ion beam to create the "Nano Trek" in 2003. This 1-billionth-scale model of the USS *Enterprise* NCC-1701-D – the starship from the *Next Generation* TV series – measured just 8.8 micrometres (0.0003 in) long!

DID YOU KNOW?

The warp drive used in *Star Trek* for propulsion is theoretically possible, based on our current understanding of physics. However, we have many scientific and technological hurdles to overcome before it can become a reality.

LARGEST GATHERING OF PEOPLE DRESSED AS STAR TREK CHARACTERS

In 2012, Media 10 (UK) rallied 1,063 costumed Trekkers to the Destination Star Trek event held in London, UK. Most wore Star Fleet uniforms, but a few alien species also made first contact, including the Borg (right), Klingons and even some tentacled monsters from the original series.

STAR TREK

What makes *Star Trek* so timelessly popular is its ability to seamlessly combine sci-*fi* with sci-*fact*. Having taken a look at the fiction (pp.40–41), we now focus on some of the real space phenomena you might discover if you were to boldly go where no one has gone before...

OUT-OF-THIS-WORLD RECORDS

1
MOST POWERFUL X-RAY FLARE FROM A BLACK HOLE
Black holes have troubled many a *Star Trek* captain... At these invisible points in space, the gravity is so strong that even light is sucked in. Every now and then, black holes eject jets of particles and radiation. Sagittarius A* fired out an X-ray flare that was 400 times stronger than normal on 14 Sep 2013.

2
SMALLEST EXOPLANET DIRECTLY IMAGED BY TELESCOPE
Exoplanets are any worlds located outside our own Solar System. 51 Eridani b is a gas giant about the same size as our Solar System's **largest planet**, Jupiter, at 139,822 km (86,881 mi) across. It orbits the star 51 Eridani, which is some 100 light years away from Earth.

3
FIRST DISCOVERY OF AN ASTEROID WITH A MOON
Generally, space rocks are at the whim of everything else's gravity, but the 53.6-km-long (33.3-mi) Ida unusually boasts its very own satellite, Dactyl. It was snapped by NASA's *Galileo* spacecraft in 1993. The mini moon (circled above) is just 1.6 km (1 mi) long and orbits Ida roughly every 20 hr.

1,284 Newly discovered planets verified by NASA in May 2016 alone. As of 8 Jul 2016, the total number of confirmed worlds outside our Solar System stood at 3,302.

4 — MOST REMOTE MAN-MADE OBJECT

No other spacecraft has travelled farther than the *Voyager 1* satellite, launched back in 1977. As of 6 Jul 2016, the probe was 20,158,370,181 km (12,525,830,513 mi) away from Earth and still relaying data to Mission Control in the USA – the **longest communications distance**.

5 — MOST CRATERS ON A MOON

The surface of Callisto – one of Jupiter's four giant moons – is 100% covered by impact craters. With its relatively low radiation and geological stability, Callisto is considered a prime target for future human exploration of the outer Solar System. Just watch out for those pesky meteorites!

6 — MOST MASSIVE "DOUBLE STAR"

Technically known as an "overcontact binary", VFTS 352 is a two-star system in the Tarantula Nebula, around 160,000 light years from Earth. They have a combined mass of around 57 times that of the Sun and orbit each other so "closely" – we're talking 12 million km (7.4 million mi) apart – that their outer regions overlap and share material.

ZOOTOPIA

Paws together for *Zootopia* (aka *Zootropolis*) – one of 2016's most watched animated movies. Audiences quickly fell in love with upbeat police bunny Judy Hopps and her unlikely partner in crime (enforcement), scam-artist fox Nick Wilde. In honour of this creature feature film, here we celebrate a few real critters that have taken to human roles like ducks to water...

$75 m

Total takings for *Zootopia* in its opening weekend – the highest-grossing debut for a Disney movie (excluding Pixar films). The previous record stood with *Big Hero 6* (2014) on $56.2 m (£37.2 m).

THE MUSICIAN

Move over Mozart – there's a new prodigy in town who's the cat's whiskers! Mindaugas Piečaitis (LTU) composed the four-minute "Catcerto" after seeing Nora the Cat (inset) playing on YouTube. The **first piano concerto written for a cat** debuted at the Klaipėda Concert Hall in Lithuania on 5 Jun 2009.

THE MINESWEEPER

In 2003, a research group led by the University of Montana (USA) found that honey bees were the perfect candidates for sniffing out dangerous explosives hidden underground – with a 98% success rate. Measuring 12 mm (0.5 in) long on average and weighing just a few grams, they are the **smallest animals used to detect land mines**.

ARE THEY *FUR* REAL?

Disney took its homework for *Zootopia* very seriously. As the film's producer, Clark Spencer, explained: "For *Zootopia*, our research began at Disney's Animal Kingdom to meet with some of the best animal experts in the world." The creative team also ventured to Kenya to observe wild animals, such as zebra, giraffes and lions, on the savannah.

Singer Shakira (COL) was the voice of the fictional pop star Gazelle in *Zootopia*, in which she performs her single "Try Everything".

THE COP

Just like Judy Hopps, Midge the chihuahua-terrier hasn't let her size stand in the way of tackling crime. At just 11 in (28 cm) tall and 23 in (58 cm) long, the K9 law-enforcement partner of Sheriff Dan McClelland (left) from Ohio, USA, is the **smallest police dog**. Her diminutive proportions come in very handy for searching small spaces, such as lockers.

FASTEST STUDIO TO GROSS $1 BILLION IN A YEAR

Disney Studios (USA) had stormed past $1 bn at the box office by 7 May 2016, just 128 days into the year. *Zootopia* led the way, debuting on 4 Mar, with strong support from *The Jungle Book* (15 Apr) and *Captain America: Civil War* (6 May). *Zootopia* alone has since surpassed its own billion milestone, having earned $1.02 bn (£775 m) by 20 Jul 2016.

THE STOCKBROKER

In 1999, Raven the chimp became the 22nd most successful financial manager in the USA! She chose which stocks to invest in by throwing darts at a list of 133 internet companies. The money returned made her the **most successful chimpanzee on Wall Street**.

JUST ZOO IT.

lululemmings

BEARBERRY

OFFICER
TRUST
POLICE

THE SIMPSONS

Homer, Marge, Bart, Lisa and Maggie have been entertaining us for 30 years. In that time, the Simpsons have amassed an impressive array of records, not to mention some of the world's most dedicated fans...

LONGEST-RUNNING ANIMATED SITCOM (BY EPISODE)

By the close of its 27th season on 22 May 2016, *The Simpsons* had aired 596 episodes. Fans were pleased to hear that a 28th season had been commissioned and was due to start broadcasting in late Sep 2016.

MOST POPULAR *SIMPSONS* CHARACTERS

Find out which Springfielders topped a 2014 poll on Dorkly.com

1. HOMER SIMPSON

2. BART SIMPSON

MOST LIKES FOR A TV SHOW

Springfield's first family are as popular on social media as they are on TV. As of 6 Jul 2016, they had 67,623,880 fans on Facebook, the world's **largest social network**.

MOST GUEST STARS IN A TV SERIES

By 22 May 2016, a total of 712 celebrities and guest actors had lent their voices to *The Simpsons* – some more than once. They include Stephen Hawking, Katy Perry, Pharrell Williams, Anne Hathaway, Danny DeVito, Glenn Close and Daniel Radcliffe (above).

MOST EMMY AWARDS WON BY AN ANIMATED TV SHOW

As of 2016, *The Simpsons*' trophy cabinet boasted no fewer than 32 Emmy Awards. The most recent gong was earned by long-term cast member Hank Azaria (USA, above) in 2015. Over the years, Azaria has voiced many classic characters, including Moe Szyslak (below right), Chief Wiggum and Professor Frink.

MOST TATTOOS OF CHARACTERS FROM A CARTOON

Michael Baxter's (AUS) back (above) is a *Simpsons* shrine, inked with 203 Springfielders. Lee Weir (NZ), meanwhile, is a Homer Simpson aficionado, with 41 tattoos of his favourite character on his arm (right). That's the **most tattoos of the same cartoon character**.

3. MONTGOMERY BURNS

4. GROUNDSKEEPER WILLIE

5. MOE SZYSLAK

DOCTOR WHO

Power up your sonic screwdriver and unlock your TARDIS as we take a record-breaking trip with the Time Lord!

3

Age at which Lily (below) began collecting Doctor Who items. It just goes to show that you're never too young to start a record-breaking collection!

POLICE PUBLIC CALL BOX

POLICE TELEPHONE

FREE FOR USE OF PUBLIC

OFFICER & CARS RESPOND TO ALL CALLS

PULL TO OPEN

WOW

LARGEST COLLECTION OF DOCTOR WHO MEMORABILIA

Fans of the Time Lord don't come much keener than 12-year-old collector Lily Connors (UK), who owned 6,641 Doctor Who items as of 20 Jun 2016. These range from figurines and props to mugs and collector's cards. Lily's ultimate dream is to one day appear as an extra in an episode of the record-breaking sci-fi series (see opposite).

Rob Hull (UK) is the owner of the **largest collection of Daleks**: 1,801 as of 25 Mar 2015, including a 1.8-m-tall (6-ft) life-sized replica. *Exterminate!*

WE COMPARE A FEW VITAL STATS OF THE FIRST AND LATEST DOCTOR

WILLIAM HARTNELL

Doctor: #1

First episode: "An Unearthly Child"

Starting age: 55

Episodes: 134

No. of companions: 10

PETER CAPALDI

Doctor: #12

First episode: "The Day of the Doctor"

Starting age: 55

Episodes: 26 to date

No. of companions: 2

LONGEST-RUNNING TV TIE-IN

Doctor Who Magazine (formerly *Doctor Who Weekly*) published its first issue in Oct 1979 and is still in production to this day. In 2016, the tie-in publication printed its 500th edition (right), featuring all of the Doctors, among other memorable characters from the show. Its design was a nod to the very first issue's cover.

MOST PROLIFIC SCI-FI TV SERIES

As of 25 Dec 2015, a total of 826 episodes of *Doctor Who* had aired, with a new season slated to run in early 2017. Pictured above is the third Doctor, played by Jon Pertwee from 1970 to 1974, with his assistant Jo Grant (Katy Manning). In 2016, the 12th Doctor was set to get a brand-new companion: Bill, played by Pearl Mackie (left).

LARGEST GATHERING OF PEOPLE DRESSED AS DOCTOR WHO CHARACTERS

On 19 Mar 2016, a total of 492 Whovians travelled through time and space to attend La Mole Comic Con in Mexico City, Mexico, as part of an event organized by TV channel Syfy Latinoamérica. The current Doctor, Peter Capaldi (right), accepted the GWR certificate on the fans' behalf.

DISNEY

The Walt Disney Company has been entertaining us on both the big and small screens since the 1920s. Here, we celebrate some of its biggest hits, old and new.

4,600
Number of computers used to make *Big Hero 6*. In animation terms, the computers were capable of running 400,000 rendering jobs in one day.

MOST VES AWARDS WON BY AN ANIMATED MOVIE

Disney's *Big Hero 6* (2014) picked up an unprecedented five gongs at the 2014 Visual Effects Society Awards, held in Los Angeles, California, USA, on 4 Feb 2015. The film's fictional setting of San Fransokyo (above) – a hybrid of San Francisco and Tokyo – contained 83,000 buildings, 260,000 trees, 100,000 vehicles and a population of 701 unique characters.

MOST WATCHED US CABLE NETWORK (CURRENT)

During the 12 months up to 27 Dec 2015, the Disney Channel won the TV ratings war in the USA. The network averaged 1.234 million viewers at any given minute, according to Nielsen data. The channel boasts many much-loved series, including *Dog with a Blog* (above) and *K.C. Undercover*, starring actor Zendaya (USA, left).

TOP 5 DISNEY ANIMATIONS

TITLE	GLOBAL GROSS
Frozen (2013, above)	$1.27 bn (£829.6 m)
Zootopia (2016)	$1.02 bn (£772.1 m)
The Lion King (1994, below)	$987.4 m (£634.6 m)
Big Hero 6 (2014)	$652.1 m (£417.6 m)
Tangled (2010)	$586.5 m (£355.2 m)

Source: The-Numbers.com; correct as of 16 Sep 2016 (excludes Pixar productions)

CONFIDENTIAL

RUMOUR HAS IT...

Disney has confirmed that *Descendants 2* is underway and due for release in 2017. It will feature new characters such as Ursula's daughter, Uma.

LARGEST COLLECTION OF MICKEY MOUSE MEMORABILIA

House of Mouse fans don't come any bigger than Janet Esteves (USA). As of 29 Apr 2016, she had amassed 10,210 items related to the fa-*mouse* toon – the **first fictional character on Hollywood's Walk of Fame**.

MOST WATCHED US CABLE TV MOVIE (CURRENT)

On the day it aired (31 Jul 2015), *Descendants* – a story centred on the next generation of some of Disney's most notorious villains (right) – averaged 6.6 million viewers. According to Nielsen, views of the telecast had risen to 12.2 million based on live+7 figures, making it 2015's most viewed cable TV movie in the USA.

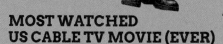

MOST WATCHED US CABLE TV MOVIE (EVER)

High School Musical 2 (2007) drew an unprecedented audience of 17.2 million on 17 Aug 2007, according to Nielsen. Live+7 figures put the telecast's total view count at 18.639 million. The movie's accompanying soundtrack also proved a big hit, earning a record for **most entries simultaneously on the US Hot 100**: eight.

WWE

World Wrestling Entertainment (WWE) has existed in one form or another since the 1950s. The blend of sport and showmanship has evolved into an entertainment empire, spawning toys, videogames and clothing – not to mention movie stars, such as John Cena and Dwayne "The Rock" Johnson. Let's get ready to rumble...

HIGHEST-GROSSING WWE LIVE EVENT

WrestleMania 32, which took place at the AT&T Stadium in Arlington, Texas, USA, on 3 Apr 2016, grossed $17.3 m (£12.1 m) from an audience of 101,763 wrestling fans – the **largest attendance at a WWE event**. Of the total revenue taken, $4.55 m (£3.19 m) came from sales of memorabilia, such as soft toys (left) – the **most merchandise sold at a WWE event**.

WOW!

LONGEST CAREER AS A WWE WRESTLER (ACTIVE)

Making his debut on 20 Nov 1990 as part of the Survivor Series, Mark Calaway (USA) – better known as "The Undertaker" – has had the longest ongoing tenure of any WWE wrestler still entering the ring. His career stood at 25 years 145 days, as of 13 Apr 2016.

29 YEARS 23 DAYS

Difference between the oldest person to win a WWE Championship, Vince McMahon (aged 54, in 1999), and the youngest, Brock Lesnar (aged 25, in 2002).

GUINNESS WORLD RECORDS

AT&T STADIUM

WRESTLEMANIA

MOST WWE CHAMPIONSHIPS WON

John Cena (USA, above) won an unmatched 12 titles between 2005 and 2014. Clearly no one-trick pony, he has also branched out into acting, presenting and singing. Cena is also the subject of a popular internet meme – "Unexpected John Cena" – which has seen his bellowing ring entrance interrupt everything from news reports to airline safety videos (see other memorable memes on pp.68–69).

The record for **most WWE Championships won (female)** is held by American wrestler Mary Lillian Ellison (1923–2007, below), who fought under several ring names, including "The Fabulous Moolah". She won eight titles between 1956 and 1999.

LARGEST ROSTER IN A WWE VIDEOGAME

WWE 2K16 features a selection of 120 current and classic wrestlers. Fans pre-ordering the game ahead of its Oct 2015 release were also given the opportunity to fight as Arnold Schwarzenegger. He appears as two different versions of his iconic movie cyborg the Terminator.

XBOX 360

W 2K16

BEN 10

For most people, the hardest decision we have to make in the morning is what clothes to wear or what cereal to eat. For Ben Tennyson though, he has to choose what life form to be!

LARGEST GATHERING OF PEOPLE DRESSED AS BEN 10

With their Omnitrixes at the ready, 475 people transformed into Ben 10 at the Red Sea Mall in Jeddah, Saudi Arabia, on 25 Mar 2016. The event was organized by Rainbow Flavoured Milk (SAU) and, as per the rules, everyone wore the traditional outfit of the TV show's eponymous character, Ben Tennyson.

WHO SAID THAT?

Record-breaking voice actor Steve Blum (also see pp.152–53) shares his experiences of working on *Ben 10*.
Ben 10 has been joyful, heartbreaking, hilarious and wonderful. I was part of the original cast, in the roles of Heatblast [above], Ghostfreak and Vilgax. Due to network shuffles, I've been tossed in and out of the different incarnations of the show for years now. A lot of blood, sweat and phlegm went into those characters and I don't regret a moment of it.

The Omnitrix was partly inspired by DC Comics' *Dial H for Hero*, first published in 1966. This comic-book featured a mystical device that could temporarily turn anyone into a superhero.

BEST-SELLING *BEN 10* VIDEOGAME

As of 28 Jul 2016, the 2007 beat-'em-up *Ben 10: Protector of Earth* had sold 4.49 million copies across multiple platforms, as reported by VGChartz. It was the first in a series of spin-off games based on the TV series.

11.65 MILLION
Total sales of *Ben 10*-themed spin-off videogames as of 28 Jul 2016.

ALIEN NATION

Who wouldn't want an Omnitrix in their life? This watch-like device (below) enables Ben to morph into thousands of extra-terrestrial life forms; theoretically, the one best-suited to a particular sticky situation, although often it doesn't work out like that! The second iteration of the device, called the Ultimatrix, contains 1,000,910 samples of alien DNA to choose from. Available specimens include everything from the moth-like Big Chill (pictured in two forms above) to the foul-smelling Swampfire and ghoulish Ghostfreak.

SPONGEBOB SQUAREPANTS

It may be Nickelodeon's most prolific cartoon (with 203 episodes aired as of Jul 2016), but *SpongeBob SquarePants* shows no sign of sailing off into the sunset... It seems the world just can't get enough of Bikini Bottom and its quirky residents!

FASTEST MARATHON DRESSED AS A CARTOON CHARACTER (FEMALE)

Donning a SpongeBob outfit, Larissa Tichon (AUS) ran the Blackmores Sydney Marathon in a speedy 3 hr 28 min 26 sec on 19 Sep 2010.

30
SpongeBob's age as of 2016. According to his driver's licence, he was born on 14 Jul 1986.

WOW

MOST KIDS' CHOICE AWARDS WON BY A CARTOON

The spongy yella fella is officially number one, with more wins at Nickelodeon's annual Kids' Choice Awards (KCAs) than any human, TV show, film franchise or game series (see more on pp.204-05). *SpongeBob SquarePants* has won 13 times as of 2016, so it's little wonder that the super-positive character always has a big smile on his face. Check out the other animated series that went up against the KCA king below.

2016 KCA FAVORITE CARTOON NOMINEES

ALVINNN!!! AND THE CHIPMUNKS (2015-)

GRAVITY FALLS (2012-16)

LEGO NINJAGO (2011-)

Many A-list stars have lent their voices to cameo characters in *SpongeBob*, including Amy Poehler, David Bowie, Johnny Depp, Victoria Beckham and Ginnifer Goodwin.

SPONGEBOB QUIZ
HOW WELL DO YOU KNOW BIKINI BOTTOM?

1. Who voices Gary's distinctive "meow"?

2. Why does Squidward only have six tentacles?

3. What kind of animal is Mr Krabs' daughter, Pearl?

4. Which American state is Sandy the squirrel originally from?

5. What is the name of Sheldon Plankton's restaurant?

(See right for answers.)

BIKINI BOTTOM AT THE TOP OF THE CHART

To date, SpongeBob, Patrick, Squidward and co have made two feature-length films: *The SpongeBob SquarePants Movie* in 2004 and, more recently, *Sponge Out of Water* in 2015 (pictured). Between them, these releases grossed an amazing $453.6 m (£295 m) at the box office.

CONFIDENTIAL

RUMOUR HAS IT...

A third SpongeBob movie is slated for early 2019; as per *Sponge Out of Water*, executive producer of the TV series, Paul Tibbitt, will reprise his role as director.

ANSWERS:
1. Tom Kenny, who also voices SpongeBob 2. Creator Stephen Hillenburg found six tentacles easier to draw 3. A sperm whale 4. Texas 5. The Chum Bucket

PHINEAS AND FERB (2007–15)

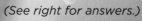

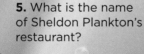
STEVEN UNIVERSE (2013–)

TEEN TITANS GO! (2013–)

THE AMAZING WORLD OF GUMBALL (2011–)

TOP 10: LARGEST MOVIE BUDGETS

You can never predict where the next blockbuster is going to come from... Throwing lots of money at a movie doesn't always guarantee that it will be a sure-fire box-office hit – apart from the times that it does, of course.

1

AVATAR (2009)
James Cameron (CAN)
$425 m (£261.3 m)

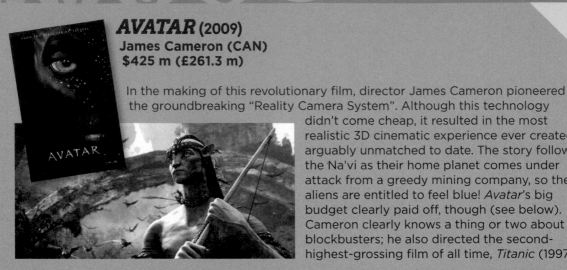

In the making of this revolutionary film, director James Cameron pioneered the groundbreaking "Reality Camera System". Although this technology didn't come cheap, it resulted in the most realistic 3D cinematic experience ever created – arguably unmatched to date. The story follows the Na'vi as their home planet comes under attack from a greedy mining company, so the aliens are entitled to feel blue! *Avatar*'s big budget clearly paid off, though (see below). Cameron clearly knows a thing or two about blockbusters; he also directed the second-highest-grossing film of all time, *Titanic* (1997).

STAR WARS: THE FORCE AWAKENS (2015)
J J Abrams (USA)
$306 m (£200.8 m)

When making one of the most eagerly awaited movies of all time, Disney could hardly skimp on the production. The ticket sales are proof that their *Star Wars* debut did not disappoint fans. As of 4 May 2016, *The Force Awakens* had realized almost seven times its budget – and that's not even considering all the tie-in merchandise.

2

PIRATES OF THE CARIBBEAN: AT WORLD'S END (2007) =3
Gore Verbinski (USA)
$300 m (£151.9 m)

Lots of gold pieces went into making the third *PotC* movie – the first of two in this top 10. The action-packed swashbuckler, starring Johnny Depp as eccentric Captain Jack, held the record for **most expensive movie** until *Avatar* came along.

SPECTRE (2015) =3
Sam Mendes (UK)
$300 m (£195.8 m)

Tied in third is the 24th entry in the main James Bond series, featuring the world's favourite secret agent. While 007 films are famed for exotic locations and luxury products, *Spectre* went the extra mile. Daniel Craig's wardrobe had an estimated retail value of £39,060 ($59,796) – making his Bond the **most expensively dressed movie character**.

BOX-OFFICE BATTLE They all had big budgets, but which of this top 10 made the most money?

$2.78 BN (£1.7 BN)
Avatar

$2.05 BN (£1.41 BN)
Star Wars: The Force Awakens

$1.40 BN (£927.9 M)
Avengers: Age of Ultron

THE DARK KNIGHT RISES (2012) =5

Christopher Nolan (UK)
$275 m (£176.5 m)

Basking in the glory of *The Dark Knight* (2008), which exceeded $1 bn (£692 m) in takings, producers invested big on the trilogy's finale. Featuring many show-stopping scenes, including aerial attacks, explosions aplenty and uber-cool Bat-vehicles, the brooding comic-book tale was the Caped Crusader's most successful film to date.

JOHN CARTER (2012) =5

Andrew Stanton (USA)
$275 m (£173.9 m)

Based on the books by Edgar Rice Burroughs – who also created Tarzan (see pp.106–07) – the story follows an ex-soldier who develops special powers on the planet of Barsoom (aka Mars). Much like the warring tribes of Barsoom, the film has both its lovers and haters, but The Numbers estimates that it did just squeak a profit.

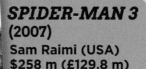

THE LONE RANGER (2013)

Gore Verbinski
$275 m (£177.7 m)

On paper, this Disney Western had all the ingredients to be a mega-hit, with Johnny Depp and director Verbinski riding high off the *PotC* series. While takings were decent, it's the only entry in this top 10 *not* to make back its budget. Perhaps unsurprisingly, then, it's *PotC 5* slated for 2017, rather than *The Lone Ranger 2*... **=5**

TANGLED (2010)

Nathan Greno & Byron Howard (both USA)
$260 m (£161.2 m)

No other CG movie had a higher budget than this modern retelling of a classic fairy tale, making it the **most expensive animated film**. By comparison, Pixar spent $200 m (£129.2 m) on *Toy Story 3* (2010), while *Frozen* (2013) cost "only" $150 m (£90.9 m). No expense was spared on technology, which proved essential for rendering all 140,000 strands of Rapunzel's golden locks. **8**

SPIDER-MAN 3 (2007) 9

Sam Raimi (USA)
$258 m (£129.8 m)

Swinging into ninth spot is the third instalment in Tobey Maguire's run as the webbed wonder. The film showing Spider-Man's darker side became not just the best-selling of the trilogy but also 2007's most profitable release. It clearly left people with a taste for more Spidey too: five years later, *The Amazing Spider-Man* became the **highest-grossing movie reboot**.

VARIOUS 10

$250 m (£ varied)

A quarter-of-a-million must be a popular figure in Hollywood, as no fewer than seven movies are tied in 10th place. The first is *Harry Potter and the Half-Blood Prince* (2009), followed by *PotC: On Stranger Tides* (2011). Next up are all three *Hobbit* films (2012–14). The budget for *Avengers: Age of Ultron* (2015) was $25 m (£16.6 m) more than the first instalment. The latest film to cost 250 big ones is DC Comics' effects-heavy *Batman v Superman: Dawn of Justice* (2016, pictured).

Source: The-Numbers.com; estimated figures correct as of 9 May 2016. Exchange rates differ over time.

$1.08 BN (£670.7 M)
The Dark Knight Rises

$1.04 BN (£677.6 M)
Pirates of the Caribbean: On Stranger Tides

You Tube

Vine

ebay™

BROWSE

VIRAL VLOGGERS

Showing off their talents, sharing advice and generally giving us a glimpse into their lives, vloggers are some of the world's biggest celebrities today. But with so much competition to be a record-breaking YouTuber, you have to find your niche...

JUST FOR LAUGHS

MOST SUBSCRIBERS FOR A COMEDY CHANNEL

The sketches of American comedy duo "Smosh" (aka Ian Hecox and Anthony Padilla) had attracted 22,347,650 subscribers and more than 5.8 billion views as of 23 Aug 2016. They previously held the title of **most subscribers on YouTube** overall (see below).

CLOSE CONTENDER

"IISuperwomanII", aka Lilly Singh (CAN), produces satirical videos based on topics such as "My Parents React". Outside YouTube, she her credits include several songs and movies, such as *Ice Age: Collision Course*. As of 23 Aug 2016, Singh had 9,675,337 subscribers.

GAME-CHANGERS

MOST SUBSCRIBERS ON YOUTUBE

The undisputed King of YouTube in terms of followers, or his "Bro Army" as he calls them, is Swedish gamer "PewDiePie", aka Felix Arvid Ulf Kjellberg. As of 23 Aug 2016, his videogame playthroughs with amusing commentary had earned him a following of 47,419,927 subscribers.

CLOSE CONTENDER

The vlog of US gamer "CaptainSparklez" (aka Jordan Maron) is one of several on YouTube dedicated to *Minecraft*; he is best known for making music videos in the game. His fan count stood at 9,501,376 as of 23 Aug 2016.

The **first vlog** is widely credited to Adam Kontras (USA). Started on 2 Jan 2000, the blog – *The Journey* – follows Adam's move to Hollywood and is still updated today.

BANG ON STYLE

MOST SUBSCRIBERS FOR A FASHION CHANNEL

Whether it's what to wear or how to apply make-up, beauty vlogging is a serious business. YouTube's current "Queen of Style" is "Yuya", aka Mariand Castrejón Castañeda (MEX), with 15,725,780 subscribers as of 23 Aug 2016.

CLOSE CONTENDER

British web fashionista "Zoella" (aka Zoe Sugg) may be behind Yuya with "only" 11,040,065 subscribers, but she can boast a best-selling writing career too. Read more about her literary success on p.98.

2,670
The most consecutive daily video blogs on YouTube, achieved by dedicated vlogger "Internet Killed Television" (aka Charles Trippy, USA) as of 23 Aug 2016.

FOOD FOR THOUGHT

MOST SUBSCRIBERS FOR A FOOD/COOKING CHANNEL

No other culinary channel has found a better recipe for success than "Epic Meal Time", with 7,025,240 subscribers as of 23 Aug 2016. Famous for its high-calorie and often outlandish concoctions, the vlog is hosted by Canadian web star Harley Morenstein (standing).

CLOSE CONTENDER

Anyone with a sweet tooth will love Rosanna Pansino's (USA) channel – a cookery vlog dedicated to baked treats and desserts, often with a pop-culture twist. BB-8 droid cakes, anyone? As of 23 Aug 2016, the *Nerdy Nummies* star had cooked up 6,898,981 subscribers.

THE BIG PICTURE

GUINNESS WORLD RECORDS

CERTIFICATE

The most views for a dedicated
Minecraft video channel
is 2,799,636,273
and was achieved by
Dan "TheDiamondMinecart"
as of 23 April 2015

OFFICIALLY AMAZING

RECORD HOLDER

Dan Middleton (UK) – better known by his YouTube moniker "Dan TheDiamondMinecart", or "DanTDM" for short – needs no introduction if you're a fan of the block-busting game *Minecraft*. He had amassed a staggering 7,943,141,552 views on his channel as of 23 Aug 2016, easily making his the **most watched video channel dedicated to** *Minecraft*. So what is it exactly about this game that has Dan hooked? "*Minecraft* is special because you can make it any game you want," he told GWR when he visited us in 2015. "You can build, go on adventures, load other people's worlds... It's just a game that does everything."

GAMES BROADCASTING

More and more people are sharing their gaming experiences with the world – and fast becoming online superstars in the process.

LARGEST VIDEO SITE DEDICATED TO VIDEOGAMES

YouTube might reign supreme in movie trailers, music videos and clips of grumpy cats, but Twitch.tv rules the web when it comes to gaming vids. As of 2016, it reported 100 million-plus monthly users.

MOST POPULAR GAMER ON TWITCH

"Syndicate", aka Tom Cassell (UK), remains Twitch's most subscribed star, with 2,457,382 followers as of 8 Sep 2016. In 2014, he became the **first to reach 1 million followers on Twitch**.

MOST POPULAR FEMALE GAMER ON TWITCH

"OMGitsfirefoxx", aka Sonja Reid (CAN, right), is the most followed female Twitcher, boasting 766,397 fans as of 23 Aug 2016. Sonja's favourite games include *Minecraft*, *The Sims* and the *Fallout* series (right). In 2016, Sonja made it on to Forbes' "30 Under 30" list of young entrepreneurs.

#4

MOST POPULAR GAMING CHANNEL FOR AN EXISTING CELEBRITY

Even those who've already found fame are jumping on the games-broadcasting bandwagon... The YouTube gaming channel "UpUpDownDown" is hosted by WWE Raw superstar Austin Watson – better known by his ring personas Xavier Woods and Austin Creed. As of 23 Aug 2016, the channel had attracted 669,493 subscribers.

MOST POPULAR FEMALE GAMER ON YOUTUBE

A self-confessed "true geek at heart" who loves to "make people smile", "iHasCupquake", aka Tiffany Garcia (USA) had 4,992,691 subscribers as of 19 Sep 2016. Her channel, which she manages with her husband Mario "Red" Herrera, focuses on her gaming adventures in *The Sims* and *Minecraft*. Other regular themes on the channel include DIY and what Garcia describes as "geek baking".

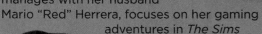

Q&A WITH... "MASTEROV"

We caught up with *Slither.io* and *Pokémon Go* gamer "MasterOv" – aka Oliver Ryan (UK, below) – at 2016's Legends of Gaming event.

Q What's the secret to being a successful games broadcaster?

A The one rule I follow is: if you're having fun, the viewers will have fun. When you're broadcasting, you need to enjoy the game and really be passionate about it. Rather than following the crowd and playing the same old games, choose something you truly enjoy, then people will enjoy watching!

Q If you were just starting out now, would you do anything differently?

A I don't think I would change anything. My channel has changed style and games over the past three years to stay fresh. I think living in the moment is the best thing you can do with a gaming channel.

Q Who are some of your favourite current games broadcasters?

A This is a super-hard one as there are so many awesome broadcasters about. At the moment I'm really enjoying the *Pokémon Go* YouTubers, as the videos are very active and almost like vlogs, so I'd have to pick Reversal, Lachlan and Ali-A.

Q What do you think the future has in store for mobile gaming?

A Mobile gaming will continue to take over the world! The phone giants are making such powerhouse devices that everyone can play amazing new games wherever, whenever.

MEMORABLE MEMES

A "meme" was first defined in 1976 by scientist Richard Dawkins as "an infectious idea or behaviour that spreads through society". The World Wide Web has now given rise to a whole new generation of "internet memes" focused on images, catchphrases and short videos that go viral online. Below are just a small selection of memorable memes that "broke the internet" and sometimes even inspired records.

1989 "ALL YOUR BASE ARE BELONG TO US"

The European version of Japanese game *Zero Wing* featured some baffling English translations – most famously "All your base are belong to us." The phrase appeared on mugs, T-shirts and even inspired a song, which itself went viral in the early 2000s.

1994 SIX DEGREES OF KEVIN BACON

Based on the "six degrees of separation" theory, this web-born challenge is to link any individual to actor Kevin Bacon in six steps or fewer. The game also spawned the "Bacon number" concept, with actors awarded a number based on their industry connections. As of 19 Sep 2016, the **most connected living actor**, according to the University of Virginia, was Eric Roberts (USA) – Julia's brother.

1996 BABY CHA-CHA

Autodesk's 3D animation of a diapered baby busting some moves was a web sensation in the 1990s. The boogie baby went on to feature in popular TV shows such as *The Simpsons* and even made an appearance in a 2015 safety video played on Delta Air Lines planes.

1998 EPIC FAIL!

The now common term "fail" is believed to originate from the Japanese shoot-'em-up game *Blazing Star* (1998), which used the phrase "You fail it!". FAIL Blog, the award-winning website, has kept failure alive and kicking since early fail videos took off. It regularly shares photos and clips of people, animals and inanimate objects in unfortunate situations.

2002 STAR WARS KID

Ghyslain Raza (CAN) filmed himself impersonating the fighting moves of *Star Wars* baddie Darth Maul from *Episode I: The Phantom Menace* (1999). According to marketing experts at The Viral Factory, by Nov 2006 more than 900 million people had seen the clip, making it one of the most popular viral videos of all time. It also inspired a wave of spin-off vids with effects added in (example left).

2003 BADGER, BADGER, BADGER

This deceptively simple Flash cartoon – featuring exercising badgers, a toadstool and a snake – was as hard to avoid online as it was to forget once you had heard its catchy song. It was created by British animator Jonti "Weebl" Picking.

Photobombing really took off in the late 2000s, led by stars such as *American Idol*'s Kelly Clarkson. In 2014, "photobomb" was Collins Dictionary's Word of the Year.

2004 "NUMA NUMA"

An early pioneer of lip-syncing videos was Gary Brolsma (USA). The web couldn't get enough of his energetic performance of the "Dragostea din tei" song, by Moldovan pop band O-Zone. His "Numa Numa" song had been seen some 700 million times as of Nov 2006, according to The Viral Factory. He also appeared in an advert for mobile network operator EE.

2012 GRUMPY CAT

A cat. Looking grumpy. A new meme is born! The miffed moggy in question is Tardar Sauce, owned by Tabatha and Bryan Bundesen of Arizona, USA. Her *purr*-pularity began with a post on Reddit in 2012 and she has since inspired a whole generation of social media cat snaps. As of 7 Sep 2016, "The Official Grumpy Cat" Facebook page had 8.7 million likes.

2012 ASTRO SLOTH

What started out as a Photoshop project by Pedro Dionísio (PRT) rocketed to fame after being posted to Tumblr. In 2015, Astro Sloth won a contest on Reddit to actually launch him into space. His picture will be in a capsule buried on the Moon in 2017.

2013

HARLEM SHAKE

The Harlem Shake is a 1980s freestyle dance, which saw a renaissance after a video was posted to the DizastaMusic YouTube channel. By Feb 2013, more than 4,000 new Harlem Shake videos were being uploaded to YouTube each day. Among them was the **largest Harlem Shake**, by American indie-rock duo Matt & Kim and their 3,344-strong crowd (above).

2014 ICE BUCKET CHALLENGE

Pouring a bucket of icy water over yourself was all the rage in 2014. It was for a good cause, though, raising funds and awareness for the neurological disease ALS – which helped lead to the discovery of a new gene in 2016. The **most people pouring ice water on their heads** is 782, set by MyIdeal Integrated Marketing Ltd and Strait Herald (both Chinese Taipei, left) on 6 Sep 2014.

2016 WHERE'S DRAKE?

Canadian rapper Drake has become a "meme machine". Some of his most memed images in 2016 were based on his *Views* album cover (left). "Mini Drake" was Photoshopped into countless scenarios, including the Where's Wally/Waldo-style scene (right), posted by Mike Squires (USA). Can you find Drake?

@SQUIRESENT

TRICK SHOTS

Beyond grumpy cats and unboxing, there's little more captivating on YouTube than trick-shot videos. Here we celebrate the kings of sport-themed stunts, Dude Perfect.

MOST SUBSCRIBERS FOR A TRICK-SHOT VIDEO CHANNEL

Dude Perfect – aka Cody Jones, Tyler Toney, Garrett Hilbert and twins Coby and Cory Cotton (all USA) – uploaded their first video in 2009. Their winning brand of sports entertainment quickly proved a hit with online audiences and, as of 23 Aug 2016, their fans numbered 11,781,047.

RECORDS SET BY DUDE PERFECT

TITLE	
Most basketball free throws in one minute by a pair (male)	35
Farthest basketball bounce shot	27.79 m (91 ft 2 in)
Most basketball three-pointers made by a pair in one minute	19
Longest basketball shot blindfolded	21.64 m (71 ft)
Most pencils snapped in one minute	57
Most ping-pong balls bounced into a pint glass in one minute	6
Highest score on the GWR football target challenge in one minute	100 points
Farthest trampette basketball shot performing a forward flip	21.95 m (72 ft)
Highest basketball shot (pictured)	162.45 m (533 ft)
Farthest basketball hook shot	21.34 m (70 ft)
Farthest basketball shot made with the head	11.32 m (37 ft 1.5 in)
Farthest behind-the-back basketball shot	10.92 m (35 ft 10 in)
Farthest basketball shot while sitting on court	16.79 m (55 ft 1 in)
Farthest blindfolded basketball hook shot	16.76 m (55 ft)

MORE STUNT-TASTIC YOUTUBE CHANNELS

LEGENDARY SHOTS

Subscribers: 243,676
This channel is all about b'ball tricks, both on and off the court. The guys have worked with some big stars, including the Phoenix Mercury's Brittney Griner.

STUNTSAMAZING

Subscribers: 772,056
Street sports lead the way on this epic sports channel, with videos covering everything from BMXing, freestyle football, pool and, yes, even a parkour pooch!

BRODIE SMITH

Subscribers: 1,522,060
What Brodie can't do with a Frisbee isn't worth knowing about... He has also battled with both Dude Perfect and Legendary Shots for the trick-shot crown.

Figures correct as of 23 Aug 2016

To achieve the record for **highest basketball shot**, Tyler Toney threw the ball from the roof of the Cotter Ranch Tower, aka Chase Tower, in Oklahoma City, USA.

Q&A WITH... DUDE PERFECT

 What's the best video that you've ever filmed for your channel?

 Garrett: My favourite has to be doing soccer tricks with Manchester City and Arsenal. As a huge English football fan, I had a blast.
Tyler: The Bass Pro Edition because we got to spend the night in my favourite place on Earth [the outdoor equipment retailer, Bass Pro in Memphis, Tennessee, USA].
Coby: I'd say a battle video but I have lost every one, so probably any of our stereotype videos. Love seeing people's reactions to those.

 Who inspires you on YouTube?

 Tons of people make inspiring content. Some of our favourites are Rhett & Link, iJustine, Whistle Sports and The Slow Mo Guys.

 Which trick took the longest to get right?

 The slingshot [right] took the longest to figure out, due to how many factors affected it.

 Outside vlogging, what is your dream job?

 Tyler: Outdoorsman who gets to hunt and fish for a living. Who wouldn't love that?
Garrett: Professional golfer. Get to play the greatest game every day.
Coby: I love milkshakes so I would be a professional milkshake maker and take my talents around the world.

 Any tips for fans looking to follow in your footsteps?

 For anyone that wants to get into the entertainer/creator space, we'd recommend doing something you're passionate about and continuing to mix it up. Don't be predictable.

11,304,417 Fans of fellow YouTube channel FailArmy (USA) – the most subscribers for a "fail video" channel. Proof that audiences love to see when things go wrong as well as right!

UNBOXING CHAMPIONS

Many are baffled by the concept of unboxing, whereby web stars film themselves unpacking products to reveal the contents and give their verdict on what's inside. But as these YouTube celebrities prove, sometimes to break records you have to think *inside* the box.

A FAMILY AFFAIR

In 2011, American father Jared (his family name is reportedly secret for reasons of privacy) uploaded a 30-sec stop-motion video he had made with his then-five-year-old son Evan using Angry Birds plush toys. Evan enjoyed making the video so much that over the next few weeks they made more. To their surprise, these videos started getting views – *lots* of views. Today, "EvanTubeHD" is one of the biggest channels of its kind on YouTube, with 3,235,021 subscribers as of 23 Aug 2016. Spin-off channel "EvanTubeRAW", starring Evan's mum and sister Jillian, is also on the rise.

MOST VIEWED VIDEOGAME UNBOXING VIDEO

A YouTube video of the *Minecraft* Papercraft Overworld Deluxe Set being unpackaged and assembled by "EvanTubeHD" had attracted 19,476,399 views by 23 Aug 2016.

Global Unboxing – SAN FRANCISCO, USA

Global Unboxing – LONDON, ENGLAND

Global Unboxing – HONG KONG

MOST WATCHED UNBOXING VIDEO

On 18 Mar 2014, "Surprise Eggs Unboxing Toys" posted a video showing off delicious-looking Play-Doh "treats" including ice-creams (above) and cupcakes. It had been seen 794,405,583 times on YouTube as of 23 Aug 2016. It's a shame you can't eat them!

DID YOU KNOW?

One of the earliest known unboxing videos to be uploaded to YouTube was posted by "Aradius Media" on 12 Jun 2006. The item being unboxed was a then-cutting-edge Nokia E61 phone (right).

LONGEST UNBOXING EVENT

On 3–4 Sep 2015, Lucasfilm staged an epic 18-hr live stream in which new *Star Wars: The Force Awakens* games, merchandise and gadgets were revealed by Maker Studios' YouTube stars, including "EvanTubeHD" (see opposite) and "aLexBY11". The event took place across 15 cities, starting in Sydney, Australia, and ending in San Francisco, California, USA.

MOST SUBSCRIBERS TO AN UNBOXING CHANNEL

Leading the way in the ever-growing field of unboxing is "FunToyzCollector" (formerly "DisneyCollectorBR"), an anonymous female broadcaster from Brazil. As of 23 Aug 2016, the well-manicured YouTuber had amassed a fanbase of 7,961,197 subscribers – that's more people than the entire population of Paraguay!

12
Countries that took part in the **longest unboxing event** (above): Australia, Brazil, Canada, China, France, Germany, Japan, Korea, Mexico, Spain, the UK and the USA.

eBUY

Could the days of the physical shop be nearing an end? These records certainly seem to suggest so... The internet places everything you might want – and a lot more besides – just a click of a button away.

ReTAIL GIANTS

Competition is fierce in the world of online shopping, with everyone fighting to sell cheaper, deliver faster and offer more variety. Over the last decade, numerous retail websites have been taken over, merged or closed down. Three of the mega-players to have endured are China's Alibaba Group and US companies Amazon and eBay. The Alibaba Group owns several eShops – including Taobao Marketplace, Alibaba.com and Tmall – with a combined 367 million users as of Oct 2015, making it the **largest eCommerce company (active buyers)**. You may not have heard of it because its reach doesn't extend much beyond China. Also based on active buyers, Amazon and eBay were the **largest online bookstore** and **largest online auction house**, respectively.

$14.83

Price paid for the first item bought on eBay – a broken laser pointer the company's founder listed. It was bought by a laser-pointer collector.

MOST EXPENSIVE POP STAR COSTUME

This outlandish jumpsuit, decorated with peacocks, was commissioned for Elvis Presley in 1973. On 7 Aug 2008 – 34 years after it was last worn by the King – the suit was sold to an anonymous collector online for $300,000 (£153,560). Presley's is also the **most expensive hair sold at auction** (right): clippings were auctioned by his barber for $115,120 (£72,902) in 2002.

EXTRAORDINARY eBAY SALES

THE ORIGINAL HOLLYWOOD SIGN	PRINCESS BEATRICE'S WEDDING HAT
2005	2011
$450,400 (£261,740)	$131,648 (£85,177)

Some people in the American south-west make a living from "denim mining" – digging into abandoned mines looking for old jeans.

MOST EXPENSIVE...

JEANS
In 2005, Randy Knight (USA) found a 115-year-old pair of Levi Strauss 501 jeans in a long-forgotten prospector's mine in the Mojave Desert. He sold them on eBay for $60,000 (£33,218) in Jun 2005. They were still in wearable condition.

SANDWICH
After her toaster miraculously burned an "image" of the Virgin Mary into her breakfast, Diane Duyser of Miami, Florida, USA, decided to put it on eBay. The saintly sandwich sold for $28,000 (£14,785) in Nov 2004. The buyer was a Canadian casino website.

BASEBALL CARD
On 6 Apr 2013, a rare 1909 baseball card, depicting Hall of Fame shortstop Honus Wagner, sold for $2,105,770 (£1,379,570) to an unknown buyer online. Wagner didn't want to be used to sell the cigarettes the cards came with, so no more than 200 were released.

PIZZA
This James Bond-themed pizza called the "Pizza Royale" was auctioned off for charity in Nov 2006, eventually selling for £2,150 ($4,072). It's not the sort of thing you normally get on eBay, but then again this was no normal pizza: its luxurious toppings included caviar, whisky-soaked steak and truffles. The posh pizza was made by Domenico Crolla (UK/ITA, below).

VIDEOGAME FIGURE
This unpainted vinyl statue of Nathan Drake, star of the *Uncharted* videogame series, was sold on eBay in Dec 2012. It was signed by the team at Naughty Dog – Drake's creators – and auctioned to raise money for the Child's Play charity. The winning bidder paid $4,250 (£2,268) for the figurine.

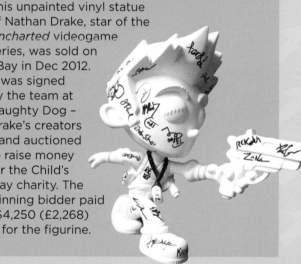

PHARRELL WILLIAMS' FEDORA HAT
2014
$44,100 (£26,323)

CLIPPINGS OF JUSTIN BIEBER'S HAIR
2011
$40,668 (£26,312)

AD SPACE ON A MAN'S FOREHEAD
2005
$37,375 (£21,719)

WIKI WONDERS

The world's largest online encyclopaedia is the go-to place for information in the 21st century. Anyone can create or edit a page, adding their wisdom to the bank of knowledge. Wikipedia contains data about everything imaginable, but some pages make up a bigger piece of the puzzle than others...

MOST VIEWED WIKIPEDIA PAGE FOR...

A MOVIE
The Avengers
(2012)

39 million views

AN ATHLETE
Cristiano Ronaldo
(PRT)

48 million views

AN ACTOR
Johnny Depp
(USA)

48 million views

AN ACTRESS
Kim Kardashian
(USA)

59 million views

Certain Wiki pages get rewritten far more than others. The **most edited Wikipedia page** is of former US president George W Bush, with 45,871 edits as of 18 Jan 2016.

5,228,208

Pages of content in the English language Wikipedia, as of 1 Sep 2016. The combined article count for the site's 293 languages is an incredible 40 million!

MOST VIEWED WIKI PAGES FOR "THIRD MILLENNIALS"

Willow Smith (USA, top right)	12 million
Jackie Evancho (USA)	4.3 million
Maddie Ziegler (USA, bottom right)	3.7 million
Mackenzie Foy (USA)	3.5 million
Lady Louise Windsor (UK)	3.3 million

Source: Wikipedia's list of people born after 31 Dec 1999; correct as of 31 Aug 2016

A TV SHOW
The Big Bang Theory and *How I Met Your Mother*

71 million views

A FEMALE
Lady Gaga (USA, b. Stefani Germanotta)

80 million views

A MUSICIAN
Michael Jackson (USA)

85 million views

A MALE
Barack Obama (USA)

93 million views

English-language Wikipedia views for the period 10 Dec 2007 to 30 Jun 2016 (older figures not available). Desktop views only

ONLINE MUSIC

The ways in which we consume music have changed almost as much as the songs we listen to... Music is at the heart of the **largest video-sharing website**, YouTube, with music vids making up 95% of its top 40 most viewed uploads, while Apple's iTunes remains the **most popular music download site**.

MOST VIEWED MUSIC VIDEO BY A FEMALE

In terms of views, Taylor Swift (USA) is the reigning queen of music on YouTube. Her 2014 hit "Blank Space" had 1,678,809,269 views as of 25 Jul 2016. It was one of her two songs in the Billion-View Club (see pp.94–95), with a third closing in: 2015's "Bad Blood" had 929 million views.

MOST VIEWS FOR AN ARTIST ON VEVO IN 24 HOURS

Songs by David Bowie (UK) attracted 51 million views on VEVO on 11 Jan 2016, the day after he died, aged 69. This smashed the previous record of 36 million views achieved by Adele in 2015. "Lazarus", the second single from Bowie's final album *Blackstar* (2016), led the way with 11.1 million views alone.

MOST SUBSCRIBERS FOR A MUSICIAN ON YOUTUBE

As of 24 Aug 2016, Justin Bieber's VEVO channel had 23,846,181 subscribers. His army of "Beliebers" had viewed his videos more than 12.3 billion times, earning him three spots in the Billion-View Club (see pp.94–95). Chart rival Rihanna (BRB, b. Robyn Rihanna Fenty), meanwhile, had 22,649,580 fans, making her the **most subscribed female musician on YouTube**.

MOST VIEWED VEVO VIDEOS IN 24 HOURS

"HELLO"
Adele
27.7 million

"BAD BLOOD"
Taylor Swift
(ft. Kendrick Lamar)
20.1 million

"ANACONDA"
Nicki Minaj (TRI)
19.6 million

In 2014, the iTunes music store confirmed that it had surpassed the 35-billion mark in downloads – the **most songs downloaded from one company**.

MOST SUBSCRIBERS FOR A BAND ON YOUTUBE

Although One Direction (UK/IRE) are down one member and officially on a break, the popularity of their channel has yet to wane, with 20,705,055 subscribers as of 24 Aug 2016. The world-conquering group's account was set up in 2010 while they were competing on the UK version of *The X Factor*.

MOST LIKED VIDEO ON MUSICAL.LY

The most popular clip on musical.ly is "#HeyNowChallenge", which was uploaded by "Liane V" (USA, right) in Sep 2015. As of 28 Sep 2016, it had amassed 9.78 million likes. Launched in 2014, the social network enables users to record and share 15-sec music videos with the world. Although the original focus was on lip-syncing and dancing to famous songs, some are now using the app to launch their own musical careers.

FASTEST-SELLING ALBUM ON iTUNES

Adele's third studio album, *25* (right), sold more than 900,000 copies on iTunes in its first 24 hr, according to *Billboard*. The singer's third studio album was released on 20 Nov 2015. The headline track, "Hello", was not only the **most viewed VEVO video in 24 hours** (see bar below), but also the **best-selling download single in the USA in one week**, with 1,112,000 downloads over its first seven days.

"WRECKING BALL"
Miley Cyrus (USA)
19.3 million

"BEST SONG EVER"
One Direction
10.9 million

Correct as of 24 Aug 2016

ONLINE MUSIC

As well as being a hub of record-breaking songs and musicians, Spotify marked its own major milestone in 2016, becoming the first music streaming service with 100 million users.

MOST STREAMED ARTIST

Boosted by the release of his 2016 album *Views*, songs by Drake (CAN, b. Aubrey Drake Graham) were streamed more than 5.9 billion times as of 21 Jun 2016. His most popular hits include "Hotline Bling" (475,260,598 streams) and "One Dance" with 409,454,354.

MOST STREAMED SPOTIFY TRACKS

SONG	ARTIST	STREAMS
"Lean On" (2015)	Major Lazer & DJ Snake ft. MØ (USA/TTO/FRA/DNK)	856,740,495
"Sorry" (2015)	Justin Bieber (CAN)	760,311,927
"Thinking Out Loud" (2014)	Ed Sheeran (UK)	720,171,176
"Love Yourself" (2015)	Justin Bieber	713,012,671
"What Do You Mean?" (2015)	Justin Bieber	703,216,980

Correct as of 16 Sep 2016

With a catalogue of 30 million songs – and some 20,000 new tracks added each day – Spotify is still king of streaming, but services such as Apple Music are catching up.

MOST STREAMED ALBUM

By 21 Jun 2016, Justin Bieber's 2015 album *Purpose* had been streamed 3.5 billion times. The singer's fourth studio album was his sixth US chart topper and sold 522,000 copies in its first week. Not bad for someone who got his start by uploading videos of himself singing along to pop songs to YouTube.

TURN OF THE TIDE?

One of Spotify's major rivals is TIDAL, a music app acquired by Jay Z in 2015. Its key point of difference is that several of the industry's biggest names are investors in the company, making it the **first artist-owned music streaming service**. Its roster of superstar owners includes Madonna, Kanye West, Beyoncé and Daft Punk. TIDAL proudly claims to offer a greater percentage of royalties to musicians and writers than any other such service.

MOST LISTENERS TO A STREAMED ALBUM IN ONE YEAR (CURRENT)

Although only released on 28 Aug 2015, *Beauty Behind the Madness*, by Canadian R&B star The Weeknd (b. Abel Tesfaye), gained 60 million unique listeners by 1 Dec 2015, according to figures published by Spotify.

32,294,391
Monthly listeners to Rihanna's music on Spotify. In 2016, her follower count exceeded the 7-million mark.

MOST STREAMED FEMALE ARTIST

YouTube's leading female in terms of subscribers (see pp.78–79), Rihanna, also boasted 4.3 billion streams on Spotify as of 21 Jun 2016, led by her track "Work" with 423,844,735. With more than 1 billion streams in 2015, she is also Spotify's **most streamed female artist in one year (current)**.

EMOJI

BLOCKBUSTER CHALLENGE
See pp.208-09

They say that a picture is worth a thousand words... So perhaps it's no surprise that the world has gone emoji mad, using the little faces and icons to communicate in texts, emails and social media messages. Certain studies suggest it could even be the fastest-growing language in the UK. However you personally feel about emoji, these records should make you 😊.

LARGEST HUMAN SMILEY
To celebrate its ninth anniversary, food and drinks company Alliance In Motion Global Inc. (PHL) put on a happy face! The supersized smiley, comprised of 8,018 people, gathered in Manila's Luneta Park in the Philippines on 30 May 2015.

OTHER HUMAN SYMBOL RECORDS

INFINITY ∞
288 people
Participants of the Infinity Campaign (JPN)

PI π
589 people
Carl-Friedrich-Gauss school (DEU)

POWER ⏻
700 people
Sathyanarayanan Venkataswamy (IND)

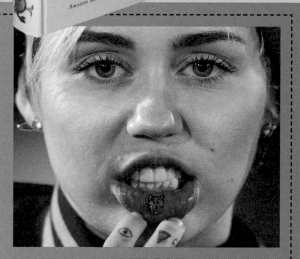

LONGEST NOVEL TRANSLATED INTO EMOJI

Data engineer Fred Benenson (USA) set up a Kickstarter project to translate the 10,000 or so lines in the 1851 classic novel *Moby-Dick*, by Herman Melville, into pictograms (example inset above). The volume, entitled *Emoji Dick*, was completed in 2010 and has since been added to the US Library of Congress – the first such book to achieve this.

ENGLISH: Call me Ishmael.
EMOJI:

MOST POPULAR EMOJI (CURRENT)

According to a collaborative study between Oxford Dictionaries and mobile tech company SwiftKey (both UK), the most used emoji in 2015 was "Face with Tears of Joy" (aka LOL Emoji). It comprised 20% of all emoji sent in the UK and 17% of those used in the USA across the year.

SAY IT WITH EMOJI

Emoji have become such a commonplace form of expression that several celebrities have decided to make them a permanent addition to their bodies. NBA star Mike Scott, rapper Drake and singer Miley Cyrus (above) are just a few to have got emoji tattoos.

TOP 10 EMOJI

#	
1	
2	
3	
4	
5	
6	
7	
8	
9	
10	

Source for Top 10: Twitter, 2015

FIRST DIGITAL EMOTICON

The first smiley using keyboard commands was typed by Scott Fahlman (USA, right) of Carnegie Mellon University in Pittsburgh, USA, on 19 Sep 1982. He proposed the use of :-) and :-(in emails to signify the emotional context of a message. The **first emoji**, meanwhile, which comprise mini faces or objects, were developed by Shigetaka Kurita (JPN) in 1998–99 while devising an early web platform for phones. He was inspired by manga and weather-forecast icons.

SELFIES

Taking pictures of ourselves has become one of the defining behaviours of the 2010s, so it's perhaps no surprise that selfies are snapping up records faster than you can say "Cheese!"

SELFIE STICK IN SCALE

LONGEST SELFIE STICK
11.48 m (37 ft 7.9 in)

TALLEST MAMMAL
Giraffe: 5.5 m (18 ft)

LONGEST SELFIE STICK

A normal selfie stick is perfect for taking a picture of you and a few friends when your arm isn't quite long enough... So imagine how many people you could fit in with a 11.48-m-long (37-ft 7.9-in) stick? Teacher Win Grau (CAN) and students from Saunders Secondary School in London, Ontario, Canada, used parts from an old hang-glider to construct their supersized selfie stick, which was officially measured on 20 Apr 2016.

FIRST SELFIE

The original photo selfie was taken by Robert Cornelius (USA) in Oct 1839, using the daguerreotype process – an early form of photography that used chemicals and a silver plate instead of film. Cornelius may have had to sit for as long as 15 min while the image burned itself on to the plate. On the back of the picture, he wrote: "The first light picture ever taken. 1839."

If you consider painted or hand-drawn self-portraits as "selfies", then they have actually been around for thousands of years.

THE DAY THE ROCK WAS OUT-SELFIED

On the opening night of his movie *San Andreas*, which premiered on 21 May 2015, Dwayne "The Rock" Johnson (USA, right) took 105 speed-selfies in three minutes with his fans. This was a record until 5 Jul 2016, when British TV presenter Nick Knowles (below right) snapped 118 selfies in the same time. Johnson went back to his Samoan roots in 2016, lending his voice to the demigod Maui (near left) in the Polynesian-themed Disney film *Moana*.

Dwayne Johnson, 2015

Nick Knowles, 2016

FIRST SELFIE ON ANOTHER PLANET

NASA's *Curiosity* rover used a camera on a long arm to capture its first selfie on the surface of Mars on 7 Sep 2012 (above right). A month later, on 31 Oct 2012, it took a series of more detailed snaps that were stitched together to form its first full self-portrait (above left).

MOST PEOPLE USING SELFIE STICKS

At a baseball game between the Los Angeles Angels and the Tampa Bay Rays at the Angel Stadium in Anaheim, California, USA, on 6 May 2016, a total of 2,121 fans wielded their selfie sticks. That was enough to knock the record out of the park!

FACEBOOK

The **largest social network** has now officially entered its teens, turning 13 in 2017. Based on its last annual report, Facebook boasted 1.59 billion active users – that equates to a quarter of all humans!

MOST LIKES FOR A FICTIONAL CHARACTER

You might think that some kind of sorcery is at work, but nevertheless Harry Potter has magicked up 75,702,196 likes – more than most real people! The next most popular Facebook profile for a fictional person is that of British comedy character Mr Bean, with 65,697,367 likes.

MOST WATCHED FACEBOOK LIVE VIDEO

One of 2016's biggest viral stars was Candace Payne (USA), but you'll probably know her as "Chewbacca Mom". On 19 May 2016, she broadcast herself live for four minutes wearing a "Wookiee-talking" Chewbacca mask and laughing uncontrollably. The video surpassed 100 million views in its first 48 hr and had been seen 159 million times by 19 Jul 2016.

MOST LIKED PEOPLE

Real Madrid striker Cristiano Ronaldo (PRT) and Colombian singer Shakira are the king and queen of Facebook, with 116,574,509 and 104,622,942 likes, respectively. This also means that Shakira is the **most liked musician** and Ronaldo is the **most liked athlete** (see his closest competition below).

MOST LIKED ATHLETES

CRISTIANO RONALDO
Sport: Soccer
Likes: 116,574,509

LIONEL MESSI (ARG)
Sport: Soccer
Likes: 86,766,871

NEYMAR (BRA)
Sport: Soccer
Likes: 58,747,961

As of Sep 2016, Facebook is the world's third most popular website according to web analyst Alexa. The only two sites that receive more traffic are Google and YouTube.

WHAT'S YOUR REACTION?

Recognizing that the Like button doesn't always suit the news or pictures that people post, Facebook released its new Reactions in early 2016: Like, Love, Haha, Wow, Sad and Angry (below, left to right). These emotions were chosen based on the emoji being used most frequently, as well as feedback from members. Facebook has said it will consider adding further Reactions if enough demand arises.

19 min 14 sec
Average time that each user spends on Facebook per day, based on estimates by Alexa.

MOST LIKED MALE MUSICIAN

He may be way behind Shakira (opposite), but among male singers, rapper Eminem (b. Marshall Bruce Mathers III, USA) is top, with 91,625,249 likes. His closest rival is Canadian pop star Justin Bieber, with 77,530,285 likes.

FACEBOOK QUIZ
TEST YOUR PIRATE LINGO, ME HEARTIES!

One of Facebook's more interesting language options is "Pirate English". Can you translate these familiar Facebook expressions?

1. *What be troublin' ye?*
2. *Captain's Log*
3. *Abandon Ship*
4. *Hoist yer flag*
5. *Skewerins*

(Answers below right)

MOST LIKED ACTORS

No other actor has a bigger fan following on Facebook than *Fast and Furious* lead Vin Diesel (USA, left), with 100,200,337 likes. This sees him racing ahead of fellow Hollywood A-listers Will Smith and Jackie Chan. The **most liked female actor**, meanwhile, is *Wizards of Waverly Place* and *Hotel Transylvania* star Selena Gomez (USA, right), with 61,375,516 likes.

ANSWERS:
1. What's on your mind? 2. News feed 3. Log out 4. Create page 5. Pokes

DAVID BECKHAM
(UK, retired)

Sport: Soccer
Likes: 54,900,015

JOHN CENA
(USA)

Sport: Wrestling
Likes: 42,383,371

All likes records correct as of 23 Aug 2016

INSTAGRAM

Nobody has mastered the art of the selfie quite like these snap-happy celebrities. They know the perfect photo can attract millions of fans!

INSTA-ART
Prisma was all over Instagram in 2016. The creative app scans your snaps and selfies then uses the captured data to transform them into mini works of art. Filters include styles based on famous artists such as Picasso, Kandinsky and Van Gogh.

SELENA GOMEZ
96,292,206

1

MOST FOLLOWERS
Selena Gomez (USA) is the most popular Instagrammer, with 96,292,206 followers as of 23 Aug 2016. Many of her posts from 2016 were snapped during her second solo concert tour, in support of her 2015 album *Revival*. Gomez and four other female stars (below) make up the social network's top five members to date.

TAYLOR SWIFT
89,414,541

2

KIM KARDASHIAN
80,534,082

5

4

3

BEYONCÉ
82,457,943

ARIANA GRANDE
82,532,960

FIRST INSTAGRAM FROM SPACE

NASA astronaut Steve Swanson (USA) posted a selfie in the *Cupola* window of the *International Space Station* on 7 Apr 2014. Its caption read: "Back on *ISS*, life is good."

MOST FOLLOWERS FOR AN ATHLETE

Cristiano Ronaldo (PRT) is Instagram's most popular sports star. The world-class striker had scored 74,069,275 followers by 23 Aug 2016, ahead of fellow soccer players Neymar (BRA) on 57,651,689 and Lionel Messi (ARG) on 51,729,138. The social-media aficionado is also the **most followed athlete on Twitter** (p.91) and the **most liked person on Facebook** (p.86).

FASTEST TIME TO REACH 1 MILLION FOLLOWERS

Pope Francis (ARG, @franciscus) surpassed the 1-million milestone in 12 hr when he joined Instagram on 19 Mar 2016. This halved the previous record set by retired footballer David Beckham, who achieved it in 24 hr in 2015.

MOST FOLLOWERS FOR A MALE

Just behind Instagram's leading ladies (see opposite) at No.6 is Justin Bieber (CAN). As of 23 Aug 2016, the multi-record-breaking singer (here pictured with his many Guinness World Records certificates) had amassed 77,901,663 fans. In Aug 2016, Bieber suspended his account, owing to a dispute with certain users. On going to press, it was yet to be confirmed whether or not this would be permanent.

TWITTER

With the world's biggest microblog celebrating its 10th birthday in 2016, we turn the spotlight on the leading 140-character celebrities.

MOST FOLLOWERS

Twitter's headline act is Katy Perry (USA, b. Katheryn Hudson), with 92,038,148 followers – that's more than the populations of France and Australia combined! In 2016, the social-media-savvy singer became the first person to exceed the 90-million milestone, which she marked with a dedicated post (below).

The **most followers for a male**, meanwhile, is 86,764,192 – for Justin Bieber.

MOST FOLLOWERS FOR A DJ

At the last count, French DJ David Guetta (above) had scratched up 20,421,604 fans on his Twitter page. This was far ahead of second-place Calvin Harris (UK) who had a following of 8,283,300.

34,573
Followers on "Katy Perry Pop Up", a subsidiary Twitter page where the "Queen of Twitter" (below) promotes products such as her own perfume.

The iconic Twitter logo is called Larry. It was named after the NBA's Boston Celtics star and Basketball Hall of Famer Larry Bird.

WHICH ACTORS TAKE THE ROLES OF LEADING FEMALE AND MALE ON TWITTER?

Source: Twitter; all follower records correct as of 23 Aug 2016

SELENA GOMEZ (USA)

Handle: @selenagomez

Joined: Mar 2009

Followers: 45,330,978

No. of tweets: 4,202

Known for: Wizards of Waverly Place (2007–12), Hotel Transylvania 2 (2015)

KEVIN HART (USA)

Handle: @KevinHart4real

Joined: Mar 2009

Followers: 30,587,133

No. of tweets: 30,300

Known for: Ride Along 2 (2016), The Secret Life of Pets (2016)

MOST USED HASHTAG IN 24 HOURS

The hashtag #AIDubEBTamangPanahon – posted by fictional TV couple "AIDub" – was used 40,706,392 times on 24–25 Oct 2015. The characters, played by Alden Richards and Maine Mendoza (both PHL) in TV show *Eat Bulaga!*, had reunited for a fund-raiser.

I'D LIKE TO ~~THANK~~ TWEET MY PARENTS...

The Oscars never fail to set the Twitterverse alight. At 2014's Academy Awards ceremony, a star-studded selfie (above) uploaded to @TheEllenShow (also see p.21) was shared 1 million times in an hour, making it the **most retweeted message**.

Meanwhile in 2016, more than 440,000 Twitter users in just a minute shared their thoughts about Leonardo DiCaprio's long-awaited win of Best Actor award (left).

MOST FOLLOWERS FOR A FEMALE ATHLETE

Tennis ace Serena Williams (USA) has netted more followers than any other sportswoman, with 6,642,098 at the last count. This was some way short of the **most followed athlete** overall, though. Soccer star Cristiano Ronaldo (PRT) has 45,642,117 fans, including Jennifer Lopez (left), it would seem!

SOCIAL MEDIA ROUND-UP

There's more to social media than just Facebook and Twitter. Here we turn the spotlight on the most popular stars of a few other social networks.

15
Age at which Lele Pons (left) first started uploading videos to Vine. In 2014, she became the first Viner to reach 1 billion views.

MOST VIEWED PERSON ON VINE

Despite being "only" the third most followed person on the video social network Vine, Lele Pons (aka Eleonora Pons Maronese, VEN/USA) is actually the most watched Viner. As of 23 Aug 2016, Pons had 8,572,853,931 "loops" (i.e., views) across 848 clips – that's more than 10.1 million views per post on average. She is also Vine's **most followed female** (see the **most followed Viner** overall opposite).

#DENIMMADEWELL

Madewell

BLUE JEANS GO GREEN
DENIM RECYCLING

TOP OF THE POPS

In Jun 2016, social app PopJam – which describes itself as an "Instagram for kids" – surpassed the 1-million-user milestone. The British app was first released in 2014 and in Aug 2016 launched in North America. The online community allows users to get creative with their pictures, offering a variety of filters and virtual stickers. The site also curates mini-games, quizzes and kid-friendly YouTube videos for users to enjoy.

MOST FOLLOWERS ON PINTEREST

Graphic designer and all-round creative Joy Cho (USA) – founder of the Oh Joy! studio – has the most popular account on the craft and lifestyle-focused network Pinterest. She had 12,780,370 followers as of 23 Aug 2016. Cho's posts, aka "pins", cover topics ranging from home decor and fashion to food.

Joy Cho / Oh Joy!

| 90 | 13780 | 21 | 12.8M | 226 |

MOST COMMENTS ON A WEIBO POST

Chinese singer Luhan (aka Lu Han, above left) posted a video about his favourite soccer team Manchester United in 2012. By 19 Apr 2016, it had received 100,899,012 comments on the social network Weibo.

At a concert in 2016, meanwhile, Luhan and 1,730 fans also set a record for **most people wearing antlers** (left). The pop star's name means "deer of the dawn" in Mandarin.

MOST FOLLOWERS ON VINE

As of 23 Aug 2016, "KingBach" (aka Andrew Bachelor, CAN/USA) had gained 16,066,791 subjects on Vine. His online caricature of "KingBach" has landed him a number of appearances on primetime TV in the USA, including *House of Lies*, *Punk'd* and, in 2016, *The Daily Show*.

©KINGBACH

TOP 10: THE BILLION-VIEW CLUB

Only a handful of the millions of videos uploaded to YouTube can claim to be part of the exclusive group to have surpassed 1 billion views: aka the Billion-View Club (BVC). Let's meet the online world's most watched stars – currently all from the music industry, bar one.

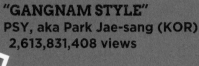

"GANGNAM STYLE"
PSY, aka Park Jae-sang (KOR)
2,613,831,408 views

1

The Korean pop song redefined what it means to "go viral", and it still holds the overall record for **most viewed video**. PSY proved that he was no one-hit wonder with his 2013 follow-up, "Gentleman", which had been seen 38,409,306 times just a day after its release – the **most viewed video in 24 hours**.

"SEE YOU AGAIN"
Wiz Khalifa, aka Cameron Thomaz (USA)
1,899,791,723 views

2

Part of the soundtrack to high-octane blockbuster *Furious 7* – the **highest-grossing car chase movie** – this collaboration with YouTube star Charlie Puth was a tribute to the late actor Paul Walker. It was the first hip-hop song to enter the BVC.

"UPTOWN FUNK!"
Mark Ronson (UK) & Bruno Mars (USA)
1,745,434,052 views

3

This catchy transatlantic tune by producer Mark Ronson and featuring singer Bruno Mars is the crowning glory of the pair's collaborative work to date. Also a hit with the critics, the track picked up gongs for Record of the Year and Best Pop Duo at the 2016 Grammy Awards.

"BLANK SPACE"
Taylor Swift (USA)
1,678,809,269 views

This is the first of the US singer's two entries in this top 10 – the only musician to achieve this feat. The electro-pop number is from Swift's best-selling album *1989*. Its popularity means that "Blank Space" is the **most viewed music video by a female artist** ever.

4

RACE TO THE BILLION

Which BVC videos reached the milestone in the quickest time?

88 DAYS
"Hello"
Uploaded: 22 Oct 2015

158 DAYS
"Gangnam Style"
Uploaded: 15 Jul 2012

184 DAYS
"See You Again"
Uploaded: 6 Apr 2015

Adele's "Skyfall", named after the eponymous movie, was the **first Bond theme song to win an Oscar**.

"HELLO"
Adele (UK)
1,647,263,720 views

The speed at which Adele's comeback single "Hello" surpassed 1 billion views was phenomenal (see bar, below). The album on which it features – *25* – was the **fastest album to sell 1 million copies in the UK** (10 days). Her first album, *21*, meanwhile, was the **fastest album to reach 1 million digital sales in the USA** (19 days) in 2011.

5

"SORRY"   6
Justin Bieber (CAN)
1,646,268,413 views

"Beliebers" have helped their hero become the first artist with three songs in the BVC – the other two being "Sorry" (2015) and "Baby" (2010). But even Bieber doesn't get it all his own way: "Baby" is also the **most disliked video**, with 6,531,515 non-Beliebers giving it a thumbs-down.

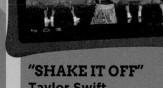

7

"SHAKE IT OFF"
Taylor Swift
1,558,285,124 views

The lead single from her *1989* album, this upbeat track continued Swift's move away from her country pop roots. It is one of her most successful songs on the *Billboard* Hot 100, debuting at No.1 and going on to spend 24 non-consecutive weeks in the top 10 – longer than any other of her releases to date.

"LEAN ON"   8
Major Lazer (USA)
& DJ Snake (FRA)
1,519,140,016 views

This Bollywood-inspired video was a collaboration between Major Lazer, DJ Snake and Danish singer MØ (aka Karen Marie Aagaard Ørsted Andersen). As well as being one of 2015's most listened-to tracks on YouTube, it has also broken records on streaming site Spotify (see pp.80–81).

"BAILANDO"   9
Enrique Iglesias (ESP)
1,513,588,192 views

"Bailando" ("Dancing") was the first Spanish-speaking video in the BVC. Released on Iglesias's 10th album, it features the song's original Cuban creators: Descemer Bueno and Gente de Zona. The English version is some way behind, with "just" 179 million views as of the same date.

"WHEELS ON THE BUS"   10
LittleBabyBum (UK)
1,507,108,274 views

One of only two BVC inductees which *isn't* a music megastar, this colourful compilation of animated nursery rhymes is YouTube's **most watched educational video**. In 2016, the LittleBabyBum channel released plush toys of some of its most popular characters, including Twinkle the Star.

All figures correct as of 25 Jul 2016

238 DAYS
"Blank Space"
Uploaded: 10 Nov 2014

298 DAYS
"Uptown Funk!"
Uploaded: 19 Nov 2014

the AMAZING SPIDER-MAN

MARVEL COMICS GROUP

12¢

40 SEPT

"SPIDEY SAVES THE DAY!"

THE END OF THE GREEN GOBLIN!

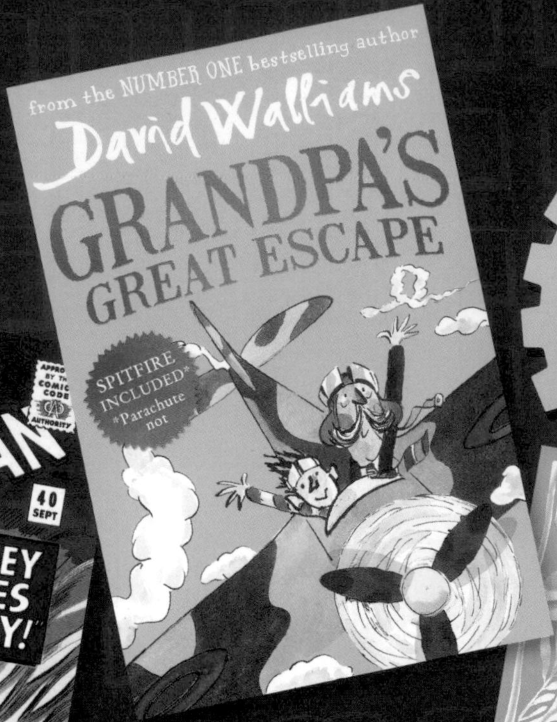

from the NUMBER ONE bestselling author

David Walliams

GRANDPA'S GREAT ESCAPE

SPITFIRE INCLUDED*
*Parachute not

JUNGLE TELEGRAPH

Despite spending many years in India, Rudyard Kipling never actually visited the jungle in which his most famous book is set.

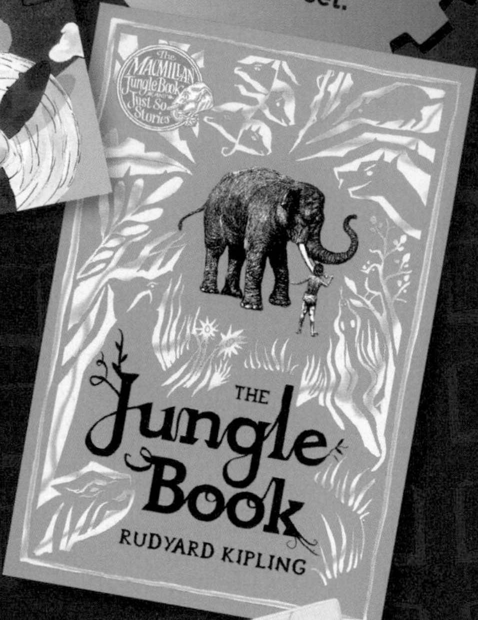

THE MACMILLAN Jungle Book Just So Stories

THE Jungle Book

RUDYARD KIPLING

Girl Online

THE FIRST NOVEL BY Zoella

READ

BOOKS ROUND-UP

Colouring and activity books may be taking over bookshops, but kids' fiction is also stronger than ever, in what some are calling a new "golden age" of children's books...

ZOELLA

With 78,109 sales, no other debut work of fiction sold more copies in the UK in its first week than *Girl Online* (2014, below) by British YouTube star Zoella (aka Zoe Sugg). Nielsen calculated that Zoella made £5.5 m ($8.1 m) between Sep 2014 and Apr 2016, making her the top-selling vlogger author in the UK. Her third novel, *Going Solo*, was set for release in Nov 2016.

BEST-SELLING FEMALE CHILDREN'S AUTHOR (CURRENT)

Julia Donaldson (UK), who co-created the *Gruffalo* series with illustrator Axel Scheffler, sold 3,036,037 books globally in 2015. Donaldson held the coveted title of Children's Laureate in the UK between 2011 and 2013.

HIGHEST EARNING AUTHOR (CURRENT)

In the 12 months leading up to Jun 2016, James Patterson (USA) earned an estimated $95 m (£70.9 m), according to Forbes. Patterson is best known for his crime books, but also pens a lot of kids' fiction. In 2016, he released the eighth title in his popular *Middle School* series, *Dog's Best Friend*.

DAVID WALLIAMS

While *Wimpy Kid* (see right) ruled the worldwide kids' book market in 2015, in the UK another title finished the year on top: *Grandpa's Great Escape* (below), penned by British author David Walliams. According to Nielsen, an estimated 615,698 copies of the tale about Jack and his ex-RAF pilot grandfather flew off the shelves, adding yet another best-seller to Walliams' growing portfolio.

Source: All book sales figures are taken from Nielsen Bookscan. "Current" refers to data covering 1 Jan–31 Dec 2015.

As well as being a huge fan of Roald Dahl's writing (see pp.114–15), David Walliams also collaborated with Dahl's long-term illustrator, Sir Quentin Blake, on his first two books.

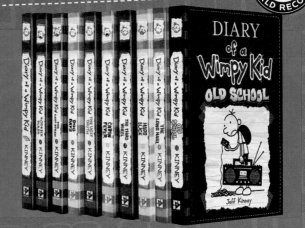

BEST-SELLING CHILDREN'S FICTION BOOK (CURRENT)

The first *Diary of a Wimpy Kid* book hit the shelves back in 2007. Ten years on, readers still can't get enough of Greg Heffley and his doodled adventures. In 2015, some 2,208,855 copies of the 10th instalment, *Old School*, were snapped up. It's little wonder that *Wimpy Kid* writer Jeff Kinney (USA, below left) was also 2015's **best-selling children's author**. Odds are that the 11th title, *Double Down* (below right), will be yet another smash hit.

Q&A WITH... JEFF KINNEY

Q Why do you think *Wimpy Kid* resonates with so many youngsters?

A I just did a world tour, and I asked myself the same question: why is it that a kid in China likes these books the same way that a kid in Brazil and Australia does? I think it's because the books are about ordinary life experiences that most kids can relate to. Most of us have parents, siblings, pets, teachers, homework – that's why the stories resonate.

Q Who were your favourite authors when you were growing up and do they inform how you write today?

A My favourites were Judy Blume and Beverly Cleary. They wrote about real-life stuff that I could relate to as a kid. I think they left a deep impression on me, because that's what I like to write about as well.

Q How much of your own childhood goes into this series and how much is purely from your imagination?

A I drew a lot of inspiration from my own childhood, especially for the first few books. Now I'm relying much more on my imagination. Sometimes, my kids' lives influence my work.

Q Tell us a little about how you started sketching cartoons and how your style has evolved.

A When I started off, I was using pencil and paper, pen and ink. I wasn't very good at it, and my drawings were very inconsistent. But as time went on, technology evolved, and now I use the computer as a drawing tool. Now my drawings are more consistent and sharper, which I really like.

Q What was it like to see *Wimpy Kid* translated from the page to the big screen?

A It was scary, really! When I'm writing a book, I'm totally in control. But to make a movie, you need hundreds of people to bring it to life. I had a big hand in the adaptation, and I was on set for about half the time on all three films. We're hoping to make more.

PEOPLE POWER: DR SEUSS

DOCTOR WHO?

Dr Seuss, aka Theodor Seuss Geisel (USA, 1904–91, above), started as a cartoonist for magazines before moving into advertising. His children's literature career began in 1931, but his first blockbuster came with his 13th title, *The Cat in the Hat* (1957, right). Although Geisel passed away in 1991, his books are as popular as ever. Nielsen estimated that 4,414,350 Dr Seuss titles sold globally in 2015 alone, putting the author only second to *Wimpy Kid* creator, Jeff Kinney (see p.99).

THE CAT IN THE HAT
By Dr. Seuss

Before his career as a children's author took off, Geisel produced adverts for a wide range of products, including oil, sugar, insect repellent and ball bearings!

$345 m
Total box-office sales of Dr Seuss adaptation *How the Grinch Stole Christmas!* (2000), making it the **highest-grossing Christmas movie** ever.

LARGEST GATHERING OF DR SEUSS CHARACTERS

In celebration of a nationwide book week in Australia, 564 pupils and teachers from St Therese's School in Essendon, Victoria, dressed as characters inspired by the much-loved Dr Seuss books on 18 Aug 2015. As you can see, the majority decided to attend as Things, but the Lorax (right), the Grinch and the Cat in the Hat (left) also put in an appearance. Why Dr Seuss? Event organizer Daniel Parry told us: "Because all his books are so engaging, exciting and entertaining. The characters are loveable, the imagery is iconic and the stories are timeless."

ALICE IN WONDERLAND

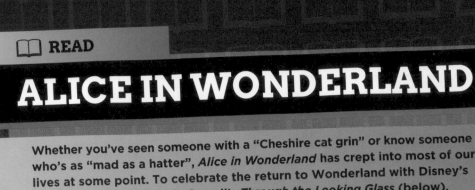

Whether you've seen someone with a "Cheshire cat grin" or know someone who's as "mad as a hatter", *Alice in Wonderland* has crept into most of our lives at some point. To celebrate the return to Wonderland with Disney's 2016 adaptation of Lewis Carroll's *Through the Looking Glass* (below), we raise a cup to some "curiouser and curiouser" tea-party records...

$1.54 m

Amount paid for Carroll's copy of an original 1865 *Alice in Wonderland* (left) in 1998. A limited first edition valued at $2–3 m failed to sell at auction in 2016.

LONGEST LINE OF TARTS

On 1 May 2015, Simon and Irene Burrows and Barry Mortlock (all UK) organized the baking of 2,045 jam tarts in Llandudno, UK – the Welsh seaside town where the girl who inspired the main character, Alice Liddell, often spent family holidays. The event marked 150 years since *Alice in Wonderland* was published.

TALLEST CAKE

In Carroll's topsy-turvy tale, a small cake turns Alice into a giant... Based on that logic, maybe eating this 33-m-tall cake (108-ft 3-in) – made by the Hakasima-Nilasari culinary school (IDN) – would make you shrink. It weighs in at 18 tonnes (20 US tons), though, so we doubt it!

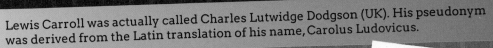

Lewis Carroll was actually called Charles Lutwidge Dodgson (UK). His pseudonym was derived from the Latin translation of his name, Carolus Ludovicus.

MOST EXPENSIVE WALL CALENDAR

A calendar featuring sketches of costume designs for characters from *Alice in Wonderland* (Dormouse pictured right) sold to an anonymous bidder for £36,000 ($57,850). It was just one of the lots at a fundraising auction for the Muir Maxwell Trust and The Fettes Foundation (both UK). The sale took place at a "Mad Hatter's Tea Party" held at Fettes College, Edinburgh, UK, in 2011.

LARGEST TEAPOT

Tea is a big deal in Morocco. In recognition of this, Sultan Tea (MAR) forged an iron teapot that measured 4 m (13 ft 1 in) tall and 2.58 m (8 ft 5 in) in diameter to mark its 80th anniversary. Presented at the International Agriculture Show in Meknes, Morocco, the titanic teapot was used to brew 1,500 litres (396.2 US gal) of mint tea on 27 Apr 2016.

LARGEST CREAM TEA PARTY

The British Consulate General Shanghai (UK) invited 735 guests for tea and scones to celebrate the Queen's 90th birthday on 14 Jun 2016. That's Queen Elizabeth II, rather than the Queen of Hearts, just in case you were wondering...

THE "KING OF QUIRK" RETURNS...

US film-maker Tim Burton (right) brought us more wacky Wonderland adventures in 2016 with *Alice Through the Looking Glass* (main picture), which he produced. Other credits in his portfolio include *The Nightmare Before Christmas* (1993) and the **highest-grossing Roald Dahl movie**, *Charlie and the Chocolate Factory* (2005; see more on pp.114–15).

REALLY WILD READS

Whether real or fictional, animals make for some of the most captivating characters – so it's no surprise that they are the stars of some of our favourite books and magazines.

2,000
Approximate number of copies of the **smallest magazine cover** that would fit on a grain of salt.

SMALLEST MAGAZINE COVER

IBM Research in Zurich, Switzerland, reproduced an etched copy of the Mar 2014 cover of *National Geographic Kids* (USA, right) that measured a minuscule 11 by 14 micrometres. Scratched into a sliver of plastic with a tiny heated silicon "chisel", it can only be seen through an electron microscope. The feat was *Nat Geo Kids*' ninth Guinness World Records title – and certainly its smallest!

MOST EXPENSIVE BOOK ILLUSTRATION SOLD AT AUCTION

In 2008, a watercolour by author/illustrator Beatrix Potter (UK) – best known for her mischievous Peter Rabbit character – sold for £289,250 ($579,232). Entitled *The Rabbits' Christmas Party*, the painting was bought by a British collector. The year 2016 marked 150 years since Beatrix Potter was born.

BEST-SELLING ADULT COLOURING BOOK (CURRENT)

Technically this is more of a really wild *draw* than a really wild *read*... In the 12 months up to 7 May 2016, *Secret Garden: An Inky Treasure Hunt and Colouring Book* (2013) – packed with animal and plant illustrations by Johanna Basford (UK, above) – sold 2,213,988 copies, according to Nielsen BookScan. In 2016, Basford also drew the cover for a special edition of *The Jungle Book*, tying in with her new title, *Magical Jungle*.

DID YOU KNOW?
The Tale of Kitty-in-Boots, a book written in 1914 by Beatrix Potter but not published because of WWI, finally hit stores in 2016. It was illustrated by Sir Quentin Blake.

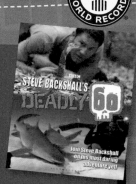

Q&A WITH... STEVE BACKSHALL

Last summer we caught up with British adventurer and wildlife writer Steve Backshall, presenter of *Deadly 60* and author of several books on dangerous and exciting animals.

 What inspired your passion for nature?

A My family. Both Mum and Dad are mad keen on the outdoors, adventure, travel and animals, and I picked it up from them as soon as I could crawl.

Q **Did you have a favourite animal when growing up?**

A It was always otters, although I didn't see one for real until much later in life. Today, it's the wolf. Always a challenge to film, yet utterly fascinating.

Q **When was the last time an animal scared you?**

A Working with Komodo dragons [the world's **largest lizard**]. We were showing how fast they run when food is on the brain. My researcher tripped over right in front of a sprinting dragon. If he'd been any closer he would certainly have been bitten.

Q **Do you think some predators get a bad reputation they don't deserve?**

A Without question. Human beings take over 100 million sharks from the oceans every year, but few people care, because they see sharks as mindless man-eaters. The change in attitude that has taken animals like wolves and otters from the category of pests to wild treasures is essential.

Q **If you were to be reincarnated as any animal, what would it be?**

A A bird. Probably a soaring vulture – without the bit of sticking my head into animal guts.

Join Steve Backshall on his most daring adventure yet!

BEAR NECESSITIES Steve Backshall shares his top tips should you ever bump into a...

GREAT WHITE SHARK

Hang vertically in the water like a human, not flat on the surface like a seal. No thrashing or stressed movements; try to keep your heart rate and breathing down. Let the animal know you can see it and it can't take you by surprise.

HIPPO

Get as far away as possible. Never get in between a mother and her calf, or a male and... well, anything really. Don't walk near African waterways at dusk if the grass nearby is close cropped as if by a lawnmower.

KOMODO DRAGON

Have a long stick to hand. Never take Komodos for granted and keep your wits about you at all times. They can look like a sleepwalking stuffed lizard, but once you've seen one really move, you'll never see them in the same light again!

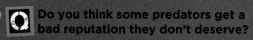

JUNGLE FEVER

Not just one but *two* classic novels with a jungle theme received lavish Hollywood adaptations in 2016. Disney's new take on Rudyard Kipling's *The Jungle Book* was first, swiftly followed by *The Legend of Tarzan*, based on the adventure novels by Edgar Rice Burroughs.

KAA

The hypnotic Kaa is an Indian rock python (*Python molurus*), which averages 3 m (9 ft 10 in) in length. These serpents don't have any venom. Instead, they lunge at their prey and coil their bodies around it until it has been crushed.

KING LOUIE

In 2016's *Jungle Book* remake, King Louie has been scaled up from the orang-utan (*Pongo*) of the 1967 animation to a *Gigantopithecus* – an extinct giant ape from 9 million years ago. Although neither animals appear in Kipling's stories, the new-look Louie is, in fact, more accurate in terms of geography. Orang-utans live exclusively on the islands of Sumatra and Borneo, the latter of which is home to the **largest orang-utan sanctuary**.

CONFIDENTIAL

RUMOUR HAS IT...

Another *Jungle Book* movie is on the cards for a 2018 release. Made by Warner Bros., it boasts A-list actors, including Cate Blanchett and Benedict Cumberbatch, and will be directed by Andy Serkis, who played Gollum in *The Lord of the Rings*.

DID YOU KNOW?

Edgar Rice Burroughs considered several names for his famous jungle hero, including Tublat Zan and Zantar, before he finally settled on Tarzan.

YOUNGEST PERSON TO RECEIVE A NOBEL PRIZE FOR LITERATURE

British author Rudyard Kipling (b. 30 Dec 1865 in India) was aged 41 years 345 days when he received the ultimate literary award in 1907. While this may not sound that young, the average age of literature laureates between 1901 and 2015 was 65. The prize came 13 years after publication of *The Jungle Book*, which inspired 2016's film (main picture).

BAGHEERA

Mowgli's wise feline mentor is often called a panther, but in reality there is no such thing. Bagheera is actually a melanistic (i.e., black-coated) leopard (*Panthera pardus fusca*). The **oldest living leopard in captivity** is Ivory (b. 23 Sep 1991), who was aged 24 years 58 days as of 20 Nov 2015. Ivory lives in Frazier Park, California, USA, and – despite what her name might suggest – is also melanistic, just like Bagheera.

BALOO

If there were a record for laziest bear, it would probably go to Baloo, but you might be surprised at quite how active this character's real-life inspiration is. Asian sloth bears (*Melursus ursinus*) make excellent climbers, strong swimmers and can easily outsprint a human. They also sport the **longest tail for a bear**, reaching up to 18 cm (7 in) long.

SHERE KHAN

Most characters in the *Jungle Book* have good and bad traits, but it's hard to find any redeeming qualities in this villain... A fellow Bengal tiger (*Panthera tigris tigris*) from Champawat district, India, is thought to be the **deadliest tiger** in history, reported to be responsible for the deaths of 436 people between 1902 and 1907.

TARZAN

Real name: John Clayton

First appeared: 1912

Adoptive family: "Mangani" great apes

Skills: Swinging, chest-beating, climbing

Inspired by: *The Jungle Book*

MOWGLI

Real name: Unknown

First appeared: 1893 (in magazines)

Adoptive family: Wolves

Skills: Howling, running, hunting, survival

Inspired by: Romulus and Remus (Roman legend)

POTTER & BEYOND

It's hard to believe that 2017 marks 20 years since the release of the first *Harry Potter* book, but demand for J K Rowling's Wizarding World is stronger than ever. On top of ongoing book, attraction and merchandise sales, 2016 saw a spin-off movie (below) and the first official stageplay – *Harry Potter and the Cursed Child* – which opened in London's West End.

A BEASTLY BOOK

Written from the viewpoint of "Magizoologist" Newt Scamander, Rowling's *Fantastic Beasts & Where to Find Them* is set in the 1920s, some 70 years before the first *Harry Potter* book. The fictitious textbook (inset) was first published in 2001. The film, with Eddie Redmayne as Newt (right), was released in Nov 2016.

HIGHEST-GROSSING MOVIE SERIES

The eight instalments in the *Harry Potter* film series (2001–11), based on the seven best-selling books, took $7,726,174,542 (£4.95 bn) at the worldwide box office, according to The-Numbers.com. This puts the bewitching series ahead of other far-longer-running franchises, including the James Bond series with 24 films to date.

CONFIDENTIAL

RUMOUR HAS IT...

If you enjoyed *Fantastic Beasts & Where to Find Them*, you'll be pleased to hear that Rowling has "already written the second [film and] she's got ideas for the third one". At least, that's according to the film's director, David Yates.

HARRY POTTER AND THE CURSED CHILD

While *Fantastic Beasts* looks at a pre-Potter era, the new *Harry Potter* stageplay – which opened at London's Palace Theatre, UK, in Jul 2016 – fast-forwards to the future, 19 years *after* the events of the final book. The play is divided into two parts, designed to be watched on the same day (matinee and evening) or on two consecutive evenings. The plot is based on an original story penned by John Tiffany, Jack Thorne and J K Rowling. Principal characters include a grown-up Harry Potter (far left, played by Jamie Parker), his wife Ginny (left; Poppy Miller) and their son Albus (centre left; Sam Clemmett).

BEST-SELLING PLAYSCRIPT

Tied into the theatrical debut of *Harry Potter and the Cursed Child*, a script book was released on 31 Jul 2016. More blessed than cursed, by 6 Aug 2016 it had sold 3,866,156 copies globally according to Nielsen BookScan, which makes it the most popular playscript since sales records began. In second and third places were two of Shakespeare's most enduring plays: *Romeo and Juliet* on 2,151,176 and *Macbeth* on 1,835,820, as of the same date. Week one sales of 847,886 in the UK alone make *Cursed Child* the fourth fastest-selling book ever, only surpassed by three other *Harry Potter* titles.

MOST EXPENSIVE CHILDREN'S BOOK SOLD AT AUCTION

In 2007, online book-seller Amazon (USA) paid £1.95 m ($3.97 m) at Sotheby's in London, UK, for a handwritten copy of *The Tales of Beedle the Bard* – a storybook mentioned in *Harry Potter and the Deathly Hallows*. One of only seven bespoke manuscripts made by Rowling, the leather tome was mounted with silver and moonstones.

HIGHEST ANNUAL EARNINGS FOR AN AUTHOR

In 2007–08, Forbes estimated that J K Rowling earned $300 m (£161 m) across the year – more than any other writer before or since. Rowling also became the **first billion-dollar author**, securing a place on the Forbes Rich List in 2004.

HAPPILY EVER AFTER...

Some of the most iconic characters from blockbuster movies and TV started life in centuries-old stories. Here we pay tribute to the wonderful world of fairy tales...

BEAUTY AND THE BEAST
ILLUSTRATION BY Walter Crane

5
Siblings Belle had in the original story: three brothers and two sisters. None of these appear in the Disney adaptation.

FIRST DISNEY FILM ADAPTED INTO A STAGE MUSICAL

In 1994, a stage musical of Disney's 1991 animation *Beauty and the Beast* (both inset above) made its debut on Broadway. The film had itself been adapted from a much older book first published in 1740, written by French novelist Gabrielle-Suzanne Barbot de Villeneuve. Proving that there is life in the story yet, a brand-new *Beauty and the Beast* movie is slated for release in Mar 2017, starring Emma Watson (right), Ian McKellen and Ewan McGregor.

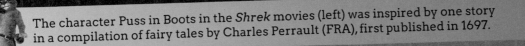

LARGEST GATHERING OF PEOPLE DRESSED AS PETER PAN

J M Barrie's classic set in Neverland inspired 289 people to dress as the Boy Who Never Grows Up, in Seffner, Florida, USA, on 30 Oct 2015. The event was organized by Rooms to Go (USA) to raise money for charity.

HIGHEST-RATED ANIMATED DISNEY MOVIE

Pinocchio (1940) is the only fully animated Disney film to earn a 100% Fresh rating on the review website Rotten Tomatoes. The puppet boy originally appeared in an 1883 novel by Carlo Collodi (ITA). The only other Disney-made movie with 100% is the part-live-action, part-animation *Mary Poppins* (1964, inset).

HIGHEST-GROSSING DISNEY MOVIE

When Hans Christian Andersen (DNK) first published his story *The Snow Queen* in 1844, little could he have known what it would inspire. *Frozen* has enthralled audiences to the tune of $1,274,234,980 (£829.6 m) since 2013, according to The-Numbers.com. That also makes it the **highest-grossing animated movie** of all time. Although Disney has confirmed that *Frozen 2* is in the works, they are yet to announce a release date; the earliest we will see Elsa, Anna, Olaf and the gang again is 2018.

LARGEST COLLECTION OF *LITTLE MERMAID* MEMORABILIA

Jacqueline Granda's (ECU) passion for *The Little Mermaid* is unrivalled. As of 16 Jan 2016, she owned 874 items, including clothing, books and toys. Like *Frozen*, this Disney animation (first released in 1989) was adapted from a book by Hans Christian Andersen.

TOTAL DYSTOPIA

Dystopias are imaginary worlds where civilization as we know it has fallen apart – and are very popular in young adult fiction today. In fact, based on the best-sellers lists, it seems that readers can't get enough of doom and gloom!

$724 m
Box-office sales for the three *Divergent* movies released to date. Shailene Woodley stars as the main protagonist Tris (centre).

WOW!

HIGHEST ANNUAL EARNINGS FOR A FEMALE AUTHOR (CURRENT)

Divergent writer Veronica Roth (USA, left) earned an estimated $25 m (£15.9 m) in the year leading up to 30 Jun 2015, according to Forbes. This means that she was tied with the established romance and thriller writer Danielle Steel (USA). The third movie based on the *Divergent* trilogy, *Allegiant* (pictured) was released in Mar 2016. The final instalment, *Ascendant*, is slated for 2017.

Q&A WITH... JAMES DASHNER

The man behind the best-selling *Maze Runner* series guides us through his inspiration...

Q Why do you think dystopian fiction has taken off in the last few years?

A I think one of the reasons is that, because of the internet and social media, we know more about our own world than ever before. And the present day is full of real-life dystopias. Fiction has always been a way of looking at ourselves through a different lens, and I think young people like to see themselves as potential heroes in a dark world.

Q Where did the idea for *The Maze Runner* come from?

A It was inspired by so many things, from the creepy maze scene at the end of the movie *The Shining*, to the book *Lord of the Flies* [see fact above], to the TV show *Lost*.

Q If you were ever dropped into a similar scenario to the Gladers, what would be your survival tactics?

A I'm not sure I'd have any! I'm such a timid chicken. I think I would have run to the corner and wrapped myself into a ball, trying to find my happy place until something killed me.

Q Tell us what it was like seeing your books come to life on the big screen (right).

A It has definitely been the highlight of my career. Movies have always been my second love to books, and to be involved with any movie would have been amazing. Add to it that these are based on something I wrote and it just becomes too surreal and fantastic to describe.

HIGHEST-GROSSING DYSTOPIAN MOVIE SERIES

No other society-gone-bad books have been more successful when adapted for the big screen than Suzanne Collins' (USA) *Hunger Games* trilogy. With Jennifer Lawrence (left) – 2015's **highest-earning actress** – wielding her trusty bow and arrow as sharp-shooting Katniss Everdeen, the four films hit the mark, taking $2.9 bn (£2 bn).

" WHO SAID THAT?

Three members of YouTube act Dude Perfect (see pp.70–71) share their tactics should they ever be picked to take part in the Hunger Games...
Coby: Cross my fingers and hope not to be picked. If I am, flee.
Garrett (far left): Run far, far away.
Tyler (near left): Bow and arrow and dominate everything. Be on the offence. "

ROALD DAHL

Gruesome, funny, heartwarming, magical... Many words have been used to describe the work of this iconic British writer. Paired with the whimsical illustrations of Sir Quentin Blake, it's little wonder that Dahl's books are so often voted No.1 among modern children's classics.

GOBBLEFUNK DECODED

One of the best-loved elements of any Roald Dahl story is his inventive vocabulary – a language that has come to be known as "gobblefunk". *The BFG* (pictured), which made a *big* impression at the cinemas in summer 2016, is a prime example. Whether it's nasty giants such as the Bonecruncher, nasty food like the snozzcumber, or "whizzpopping", which is, well, something else that's rather nasty... Dahl has a way of always getting across exactly what he means.

17
Children's books written by Dahl. His first was *The Gremlins* (1943) and his last was *The Minpins* (1991).

THE BFG IN SCALE
How tall is the Big Friendly Giant? See how he stacks up to some high-reaching record holders...

TALLEST DOG EVER
Zeus (USA):
1.118 m (3 ft 8 in)

TALLEST MAN EVER
Robert Wadlow (USA):
2.72 m (8 ft 11.1 in)

TALLEST MAMMAL
Giraffe:
5.5 m (18 ft)

THE BFG
7.3 m (24 ft)

Roald Dahl also penned a number of screenplays for film – one of the most famous being the classic musical *Chitty Chitty Bang Bang* (1968).

MOST LAURENCE OLIVIER AWARD WINS

In 2012, the Royal Shakespeare Company's *Matilda the Musical*, based on Dahl's tale of a girl who develops telekinetic powers, won seven Olivier awards. (The stage adaptation of Mark Haddon's *The Curious Incident of the Dog in the Night-Time* matched this feat a year later.) The Best Actress gong was shared by four girls who played Matilda at various ages; one of the lead stars, Eleanor Worthington-Cox (UK), became the **youngest Olivier winner**, aged 10.

HIGHEST-GROSSING ROALD DAHL MOVIE ADAPTATION

Charlie and the Chocolate Factory (2005, main picture) has been the most successful of the books by Dahl to have received the big-screen treatment. The film, starring Johnny Depp as the eccentric Willy Wonka (left), took a sweet $475,825,484 (£276.2 m) globally; see the closest contenders in the table below.

TOP 5 DAHL ADAPTATIONS

Charlie and the Chocolate Factory (2005)	$475.8 m (£276.2 m)
The BFG (2016)	$139.9 m (£106.9 m)
Fantastic Mr Fox (2009, above left)	$47 m (£30.8 m)
Matilda (1996)	$33 m (£24.1 m)
James and the Giant Peach (1996, left)	$28.9 m (£15.4 m)
Source: The-Numbers.com; correct as of 23 Aug 2016	

PAST PERILS

From "golden ages" to the "good old days", there can be a tendency to look at history through rose-tinted glasses. But let's make no bones about it – the past could be a pretty horrifying place!

8,000
Estimated gladiators who died per year across the Roman Empire in combat or during training in schools such as the Ludus Magnus (below).

LARGEST GLADIATOR SCHOOL

Able to hold 3,000 spectators, the Ludus Magnus – aka the Great Gladiator School – was the biggest of four in ancient Rome where gladiators trained. A tunnel linked the building directly to the Colosseum (above), in which they fought. Russell Crowe (left) famously played the lead role in *Gladiator* (2000), the **highest-grossing gladiator movie**.

LARGEST OUTBREAK OF DANCING MANIA

Imagine not being able to stop dancing! That's the main symptom of a condition called tarantism, or dancing mania. The most widespread case reported occurred in Aachen, Germany, in Jul 1374, when thousands of people are said to have broken into a frenzied jig for several hours. It was once thought to be caused by a spider bite, but this has never been confirmed.

OLDEST ICE BODY

In 1991, the mummy of a Neolithic man was discovered in a melting glacier on the Italian-Austrian border, some 5,300 years after he died. Analysis of the man, dubbed Ötzi (shown right, alongside a reimagined model of what he may have looked like), revealed that he had likely been killed by an arrowhead found in his back. Ötzi is also the owner of the world's **oldest tattoos**.

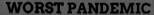

WORST PANDEMIC

If you're ever feeling sorry for yourself when you've got a cold, spare a thought for the people of the mid-14th century. They had to contend with the plague, aka the Black Death. The super-contagious bug – which was passed on by fleas from rats – is estimated to have wiped out 75 million people.

Q&A WITH... TERRY DEARY

One man who knows a thing or two about history's dark side is Terry Deary (UK), author of the best-selling *Horrible Histories* books...

Q What makes *Horrible Histories* (*HH*) so timelessly popular?

A Everyone loves quirky or unusual facts. *HH*, like the *Guinness World Records* books, explore the amazing behaviour of human beings. They have us laughing, gasping, cringing and asking, "Did someone REALLY do that?" The past was not a pleasant place to live. It was dirty and dangerous, cruel and crude, with foul food and even more terrible toilets. It's fascinating to read about the old days... we are just glad we don't have to live there.

Q Who is the most villainous person you've ever written about?

A My pet hate is King Henry VIII. A deplorable man and a perfect example of why we should never put so much power in the hands of a single person. His daughters Mary and Elizabeth were nearly as bad.

Q If you were to write a *HH* book about the 21st century, what might you include?

A There are so many rotten rulers, cruel crimes and painful punishments in this world. There have been dreadful disasters and we live in a world of wars, poverty and plagues. In fact, modern misery is every bit as grim as history's horrors. Some things never change.

Q With *HH* books, TV series, stage plays and more, there must be scope for a movie. If you could cast yourself, who would you play?

A I would want to be the world's greatest hero (well, it is *my* film), so I would want to be a common man in the endless struggle against privilege and power. I'd play the part I was born to play and always will play... I'd be Mr Peasant. I wouldn't have a name that has gone down in history, like Churchill or Napoleon, Cleopatra or Victoria. Of course, I'd end up dead, but it is better to die on your feet than live on your knees.

Q Your *Fire Thief* trilogy is a departure from historical fact for mythology. Was this a welcome change?

A I've published 280 books and more than half are fiction. *HH* are fun to write, but I'd written 50 children's novels before I turned to non-fiction. Fiction is my first love and I still publish about 10 new fiction titles each year.

THE BIG PICTURE

With his first collection of stories published in 1926, Winnie the Pooh celebrated his 90th birthday in 2016. Of course, Pooh Bear and gang have long since moved beyond the pages of A A Milne's (UK) books, as the home of Deb Hoffmann in Waukesha, Wisconsin, USA, confirms... With 13,213 items as of 18 Oct 2015, hers is the **largest collection of Winnie the Pooh memorabilia**. Asked if there's a day she'll ever stop collecting, she told us adamantly, "When I don't have a pulse any more, I'll be done. When I'm at the big honey pot in the sky, they better have a really big museum, because they're going to have a truckload of Winnie the Poohs coming up!"

"I've actually had people ask me for my autograph... It always makes me feel so honoured to almost be the Winnie the Pooh ambassador." *Deb Hoffmann*

COMIC BOOKS ROUND-UP

Superheroes have made themselves so at home on the big screen that it's easy to forget where they started out. Here the colourful comic books that gave rise to the legends – and their makers – get their well-deserved spell in the spotlight!

550,467 Orders of the debut edition of Marvel's *Secret Wars* – the second-best-selling issue of a comic book in 2015, according to Diamond Comic Distributors.

LARGEST PUBLISHER OF COMICS (CURRENT)

In 2015, comic books by Marvel (USA) made up 41.82% of units sold to shops worldwide, according to the wholesaler Diamond Comic Distributors. As well as classic franchises such as *X-Men*, *Avengers* and *Guardians of the Galaxy*, the publisher also introduced a brand-new series set in a galaxy far, far away… *Star Wars* issue #1 (left) proved such a hit that it became 2015's **best-selling issue of a comic book**, with an estimated 1,073,027 orders.

LONGEST CAREER AS A COMIC-BOOK ARTIST

Iconic comics artist Al Jaffee (USA) has been in the trade longer than anyone. Since his first publication in *Joker Comics* in Dec 1942 through to the Apr 2016 issue of *MAD* – his career had lasted 73 years 3 months.

LONGEST-RUNNING WEEKLY COMIC

Home to Dennis the Menace and his dog, Gnasher, *The Beano* was launched on 30 Jul 1938 by D C Thomson (UK) and has been published weekly ever since. The only exception was a period during World War II, when the UK was hit by paper shortages. As of 25 Jun 2016, the comical comic book was on issue #3,840.

LARGEST PUBLISHER OF MANGA

Shueisha, Inc. – founded in Tokyo, Japan, in 1925 – holds an estimated 30% share of the country's manga market. Its flagship title is *Weekly Shōnen Jump* – in which *Dragon Ball*'s Goku (right) made his debut. In Sep 2014, *Shōnen Jump* had a circulation of 2.7 million, the **most copies of a manga published in a year**.

FASTEST TIME TO PRODUCE A COMIC BOOK

As any comic-book artist will tell you, going from first concept to final comic can be a long and difficult journey. This wasn't the case for the 24-page *Nobody Goes Down to RoboTown*, however. It came together in just 11 hr 15 min 38 sec at the Amazing Arizona Comic Con on 25 Jan 2014. Creators Jesse James Criscione (above left) and Shawn Demumbrum (above right; both USA) led a team of 115 artists, also earning the record for **most contributors to a published comic book** in the process.

MARVELS OF MARVEL

If there were a fantasy football-style game for Marvel beings, the first thing you'd want to check out is Marvel's official Powergrid. These ratings assess each character by six key qualities on a seven-point scale. Assembled here are just two teams that, were they to join forces, would max out the Powergrid, with all members scoring 7 out of 7. Who would be on *your* ultimate Marvel team?

STRENGTH

Ability to lift 100+ tons

Thor
In addition to super-dense bones and flesh – and, of course, an awesome hammer – this Asgardian god can channel his father's "Odinforce" to boost all of his abilities.

DURABILITY

Virtually indestructible

The Hulk
Bruce Banner's angry green alter ego has withstood everything from poison to mind-control and even nuclear bombs.

FIGHTING SKILLS

Master of combat

Lady Deathstrike
Like Wolverine, this Japanese cyborg has bones coated in adamantium. She is a martial arts expert and is particularly deadly with a sword and claws.

THE BACK-UP TEAM

CAPTAIN BRITAIN

Captain America's transatlantic counterpart, Brian Braddock, not only has superhuman strength but also advanced senses and the ability to fly.

JUGGERNAUT

After touching a mystical gem, Cain Marko was never the same again. Once Juggernaut gets moving, nothing can stand in his way.

HAWKEYE

Nobody can match Clint Barton's skill with a bow and arrow. In fact, his marksmanship using any range weapon is unrivalled.

INTELLIGENCE

Omniscience (all-knowing)

Emma Frost
As if being able to turn your body into diamond weren't enough, the White Queen is also one smart cookie. She has put her mental and telepathic abilities to use as a businesswoman and as the leader of the Hellfire Club.

SPEED

Warp speed (faster than light)

Nightcrawler
With the ability to teleport, this gentle-hearted blue mutant can transport himself and others anywhere he can see quicker than you can say "Bamf!"

ENERGY PROJECTION

Virtually unlimited command of all energy

Silver Surfer
Using cosmic forces, this alien from the world of Zenn-La can control objects at an atomic level. He converts matter into energy for both attack and defence.

PROFESSOR X

The founder of the X-Men, Charles Xavier is one of the most powerful telepaths ever in the Marvel universe.

JEAN GREY

Professor X's protégé can control minds, move objects and create force-fields all with her brain. She is even more potent when she turns into the Phoenix.

QUICKSILVER

Magneto's son moves so fast that he can actually travel into the future by several days! His twin sister is the Scarlet Witch.

TOP 10: KIDS' BOOK VILLAINS

For 2016's World Book Day, 7,000 readers of all ages voted for their favourite heroes and villains from children's literature. These were the villainous results...

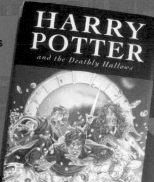

1

LORD VOLDEMORT

Harry Potter series
20.30%

He Who Must Not Be Named clearly left his (dark) mark on plenty of readers because he ran away with more than a fifth of the vote! You Know Who's terrifying return from beyond the grave – aided by his devilish minions, the Death Eaters – made him the most memorable fictional villain in children's books. It's a testament to J K Rowling's popularity that, as well as two other baddies (see Nos.2 and 6), two *Harry Potter* characters also made it into the list of top 10 heroes (see top right).

2

DOLORES UMBRIDGE

Harry Potter series
12.64%

This kitten-loving witch with a predilection for pink may look sweet and innocent on the surface, but as all *Harry Potter* readers know, that couldn't be any further from the truth. With her tortuous punishments and plain annoying sense of self-righteousness, it's little wonder that she ranked as the most evil villainess in this top 10.

3

CRUELLA DE VIL

The Hundred and One Dalmatians
8.44%

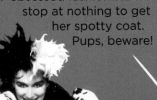

Dodie Smith's Cruella De Vil is definitely a dog person – just not in the usual sense... This fur-obsessed fashionista will stop at nothing to get her spotty coat. Pups, beware!

4

THE WHITE WITCH

The Lion, The Witch and The Wardrobe
7.40%

Jadis the White Witch from the *Chronicles of Narnia* series, by British children's author C S Lewis, ended up in Narnia after killing every single inhabitant of her own world, Charn. Her first action in her new home was to attack its kindly feline ruler, Aslan, with a big stick. Talk about making a bad first impression!

MISS TRUNCHBULL
5

Matilda
6.60%

Agatha Trunchbull, the fearsome headmistress of Crunchem Hall Primary School in Roald Dahl's 1988 novel *Matilda*, despises children. She hates them so much that she has convinced herself she was never a child herself. Not a promising background for a teacher...

BELLATRIX LESTRANGE
6

Harry Potter series
5.06%

Sirius Black's evil cousin (and Draco Malfoy's aunt) is one of Voldemort's most feared allies. She's a vicious killer who bumps off several of Harry Potter's closest friends single-handed – or should that be single-wanded?

BILL SIKES
7

Oliver Twist
4.93%

Taking a break from fantasy baddies, No.7 is the most believably real of all the villains on this list. Bill Sikes is a violent career criminal who recruits the young Oliver Twist to help him pick a pocket or two. The tale's author, Charles Dickens, worked as a journalist in London, UK, and probably based Sikes on the scary offenders he met in court.

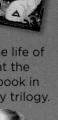

GRAND HIGH WITCH
8

The Witches
3.79%

Distinguished by her big nose, long claws (covered by gloves) and bald head (covered by a wig), the Grand High Witch is the leader of the world's evil sorceresses. Dahl's 1983 novel revolves around her dastardly plan to turn all children into mice.

COUNT OLAF
9

A Series of Unfortunate Events series
3.66%

A crazy criminal mastermind, Count Olaf spends 13 books – by Lemony Snicket (aka Daniel Handler) – trying to steal the Baudelaire children's inheritance after their parents mysteriously die. He is a skilled con-artist who loves to don a disguise, but his schemes often fall back on his favourite pastime: starting fires.

MRS COULTER
10

His Dark Materials series
2.62%

Stylish and glamorous Marisa Coulter sweeps into the life of young Lyra Belacqua at the beginning of the first book in Philip Pullman's fantasy trilogy. The motives of this cunning, power-driven woman are never entirely clear, but her ruthless streak must not be underrated.

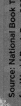

Source: National Book Tokens for World Book Day, 2016

42.5 MILLION

PS4s sold as of 1 Aug 2016, making it the best-selling eighth-gen games console. Its main rival, the Xbox One, had sold 21.84 million as of the same date.

PLAY

BRICKTOPIA

BLOCKBUSTER
CHALLENGE
See pp.208–09

No matter whether you're a fan of animals, buildings, spaceships, ninjas, pirates, princesses, superheroes – or just about anything, really – everyone's going loco for LEGO®. The world's **largest construction toy brand** offers infinite 3D-construction possibilities.

GO FIGURE!

Since 1978, more than 4 billion LEGO Minifigures have been made. If they were human, they would be the biggest population group on the planet!

FARTHEST DISTANCE TRAVELLED BY LEGO MINIFIGURES

Three special LEGO Minifigures made of space-grade aluminium voyaged to Jupiter, a 2.8-billion-km (1.74-billion-mi) trip from Earth. The trio take the form of Roman gods Jupiter and Juno (left and centre), plus the 17th-century Italian scientist Galileo (right). They are on board NASA's *Juno* probe, the **most distant solar-powered spacecraft**, which in Jul 2016 descended into Jupiter's orbit – the closest we have ever come to the planet.

30,000

LEGO Minifigures included in the Allianz Arena model at LEGOLAND. The actual stadium can accommodate more than double that, with a 75,000 capacity.

Duncan Titmarsh's top tips for LEGO builders are to "practise curves in all directions" and to "keep building different models, even when you don't feel like it".

LARGEST LEGO BRICK MAMMOTH AND MOA

Not even extinct beasts are beyond the scope of LEGO creators, as proven by these mighty megafauna. The mammoth stood 2.47 m (8 ft 1 in) high, while the moa bird was even taller at 3.17 m (10 ft 4.8 in). These prehistoric-themed sculptures were built by Bright Bricks, led by Duncan Titmarsh (both UK), on 1 Nov 2015. Duncan, who is the UK's only LEGO Certified Professional (more LCPs on pp.130–31), told us: "The biggest challenge [with the mammoth] was doing the head, as it had to hang off a bit of steel and the bricks had to line up with the rest of the body."

MOST EXPENSIVE LEGO MINIFIGURE ACCESSORY

In Feb 2014, Andre Hurley (USA) paid a far-from-mini $15,000 (£8,955) for a unique platinum Avohkii Mask of Light (right), based on a now-discontinued LEGO BIONICLE line. Hurley already owned a 14-carat-gold Kanohi Hau mask, so his exclusive collection is growing!

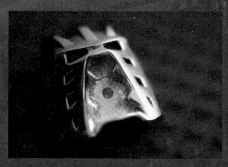

LARGEST LEGO BRICK SCULPTURE OF A REAL-LIFE STADIUM

In 2005, LEGOLAND Deutschland Resort in Günzburg, Germany, unveiled a 1:50-scale replica of the Allianz Arena football stadium in Munich. It is 5 m (16 ft 4 in) long, 4.5 m (14 ft 9 in) wide and 1 m (3 ft 3 in) tall and is comprised of more than 1 million bricks. Great pains were taken to ensure attention to detail, making use of the arena's original blueprints from the Swiss architects Herzog & de Meuron.

WOW!

MASTER BUILDERS

Decided what you want to be when you grow up? Once you've heard what these LEGO® Certified Professionals (LCPs) have to say, you may have a new career plan...

Q&A WITH... NATHAN SAWAYA

Nationality: USA
Known for: The Art of the Brick exhibition

 What first drew you to LEGO?

 I've been a full-time artist creating with LEGO bricks for more than a decade. Prior to that, I was playing with LEGO just like millions of other fans. I liked how it could be anything I could imagine. If I wanted to be an astronaut, I built myself a rocket ship. If I wanted to be a rock star, I built myself a guitar...

 Which has been the most challenging model you've built?

 There are some pretty big works in my portfolio, including a 20-ft-long [6.1-m] *T. rex* [above right] – the **largest LEGO brick skeleton**. But I'd have to say the most challenging has been my take on a life-size Batmobile [below]. It tours the globe as part of The Art of the Brick: DC Comics exhibition.

The sculpture is over 18 ft [5.4 m] long and weighs 1,500 lb [680 kg].

 What are you up to in 2016?

 It's going to be a great year; plans so far include an array of projects that range from Superman, Batman and Wonder Woman, to interpretive and abstract art, to a host of international travel.

 Any tips for budding LEGO professionals?

 Don't get discouraged. Have patience. Creating large LEGO sculptures can take time, but also remember to have fun. There is no wrong way to create art.

Do you have a favourite LEGO Minifigure?

I do; I created it myself. It has Batman's cape and cowl, Darth Vader's head and the body of Santa. I call it Darth Bat Claus.

Q&A WITH... ANDY HUNG

Nationality: Hong Kong, China
Known as: Only LCP in China

How were you introduced to LEGO?

My first set was an airport model that I got when I was five. As I loved it so much, my parents gave me a box-set when I had a good exam result or as a gift during festivals.

What was the first model you made after becoming a certified professional?

My first sculpture was a hotel in Macau called Studio City [below left], with dimensions of around 3 x 3 x 1.7 m [9 ft 10 in x 9 ft 10 in x 5 ft 6 in]. It was built with my team over about two months – special thanks to Alex Hui! It used over 1 million components.

Which has been the toughest model?

I was asked to create some of the Forbidden City's most iconic buildings by the Macau Museum of Art. The final model used more than 600,000 pieces. It was especially challenging to capture the intricate design.

Any tips for new builders?

Pay attention to your surroundings; try something new; be yourself and you will find your own style.

Q&A WITH... RYAN McNAUGHT

Nationality: Australia
Known as: The BrickMan

Why is LEGO so timeless?

It is timeless as it is "trend agnostic", meaning that it can go with all trends by being so flexible. For example, if a child is into cars, they can build lots of cars; if the next month the child is into superheroes, they can make superheroes. The same blocks can become literally anything as children grow up and their tastes change.

What was the first sculpture you made as a certified professional?

A 250,000-brick cruise ship from the 1980s TV show called *The Love Boat*. It's a cutaway model, so you can see what is happening inside throughout the ship.

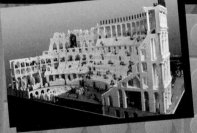

Which has been the most challenging model?

A model of the Colosseum [above]. LEGO bricks are square and rectangular, while this ancient monument is oval, so it was quite a challenge!

Which character from *The LEGO Movie* do you most relate to?

Probably Lord Business [left], because sometimes I have to use the Kragle!

VIRTUAL BRICKS

If you thought that the scope to create was endless with real LEGO® bricks, you can only marvel at the possibilities in a digital world... The 68 LEGO-themed videogames released to date easily make it the **most prolific videogame series based on a toy.**

20
Years since the first LEGO videogame, *LEGO Island*, was released. The PC game's lead character was a pizza-delivery boy called Pepper Roni.

FASTEST TIME TO ASSEMBLE THE STARTER-PACK CHARACTERS IN *LEGO DIMENSIONS*

Leon Ip (UK) built Batman, Gandalf and Wyldstyle and then spawned them into the 2015 videogame in a lightning-quick 32 sec on 9 Jan 2016. Leon also set another *LEGO Dimensions* record for the **fastest time to build the Batmobile,** completing the car in 1 min 13 sec on 4 Mar 2016.

DETECTING RELIC

BEST-SELLING LEGO VIDEOGAMES

TITLE	SALES (millions)
LEGO Star Wars: The Complete Saga (2007)	15.72
LEGO Batman: The Videogame (2008)	13.64
LEGO Indiana Jones: The Original Adventures (2008)	12.05
LEGO Marvel Super Heroes (2013)	9.76
LEGO Harry Potter: Years 1–4 (2010, right)	8.50
Source: VGChartz.com; correct as of 9 Aug 2016	

LEGO Star Wars: The Force Awakens also included exclusive story levels that revealed events that took place off-screen in the film, such as how C-3PO ended up with a replacement arm.

TALLEST LEGO MODEL IN A VIDEOGAME

For developer TT Games (UK), the first step when creating a new LEGO game is sitting down and playing with LEGO bricks. Every item and setting is assembled by a team of master builders before it is scanned and digitally recreated in-game. As of 21 Oct 2015, Barad-dur Tower in *LEGO The Lord of the Rings* (2013) was the tallest structure that the team had built. The eerie edifice was 2.5 m (8 ft 2 in) high and used 53,673 bricks.

MOST PROLIFIC DEVELOPER OF TOY VIDEOGAMES

LEGO Star Wars: The Force Awakens (below), released on 28 Jun 2016, is the 30th LEGO videogame by TT Games. Including their 2007 release *Transformers: The Game*, it brings the developer's total toy-themed games to 31. Their record-setting partnership with LEGO has seen them create hugely successful videogames of several blockbuster movies, including the *Harry Potter* series and *Avengers* (right).

A FORCE TO BE RECKONED WITH...

TT Games first brought LEGO and *Star Wars* together in 2005, creating one of today's most popular gaming franchises. The latest instalment is their take on *The Force Awakens* (left), released in Jun 2016. GWR's Adam Millward (right) attended the launch of *LEGO Star Wars: The Force Awakens* and caught up with the game's director, Jamie Eden (far right). "*The Force Awakens* is really well paced in terms of how the film can be adapted to a game," Jamie told us. "It's all action, or it's introducing new and interesting characters." He added that his team had worked especially hard to give players more freedom than ever before, with "3D flight" sections and "Multi-Builds". Jamie describes the latter as "piles of LEGO bricks that you can smash and rebuild into different configurations, just like physical bricks".

COOL CONSTRUCTIONS

LEGO bricks aren't the only toy out there for making amazing sculptures – there's a whole world of construction possibilities just waiting to be built...

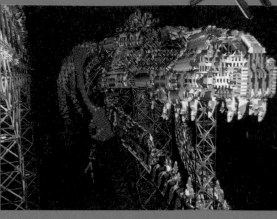

LARGEST K'NEX BALL MACHINE

Austin Granger (USA) used 126,285 pieces to construct his captivating K'NEX contraption on which a ball travels 278 m (912 ft) through a series of complex connected elements. Housed at The Works Museum in Bloomington, Minnesota, USA, the machine was verified on 13 Mar 2016.

LARGEST K'NEX SKELETON

This K'NEX dino, affectionately known as "K'REX", is the largest replica of a skeleton made out of the colourful rod-and-connector toy – comprising around 141,950 pieces in all! Created by Space Camp crew trainers at the US Space & Rocket Center in Huntsville, Alabama, USA, the multicoloured monster stands 3.8 m (12 ft 5 in) tall and 10.2 m (33 ft 5 in) long – that's almost the length of a double-decker bus!

LARGEST CARDBOARD SCULPTURE

Proving that you don't always need pre-made toys to realize your creative building projects, the D•Park mall (CHN) made a 103.1-m² (1,109.7-sq-ft) castle-themed maze completely out of cardboard in Kowloon, Hong Kong, China. Local art students also decorated the record-breaking fortress with various scenes, featuring children, animals and flowers. The castle was erected to celebrate the mall's official opening on 4 Apr 2016.

Meccano is one of the world's oldest construction toys. It launched in 1901 – a total of 48 years before the first LEGO bricks hit the market and 91 years before K'NEX arrived.

LARGEST K'NEX SCULPTURE

The *Bloodhound SSC* is a supersonic car hoping to break the 1,000-mph (1,600-km/h) barrier. Although that goal is yet to be realized, a life-size replica of the car has already set a mega K'NEX record. Assembled by the BLOODHOUND SSC RBLI K'NEX Build Team (UK), the model measures 13.38 m (43 ft 10.7 in) long and 3.87 m (12 ft 8.3 in) tall, and comprises in excess of 350,000 pieces.

LARGEST MECCANO STRUCTURE

Queen's University and local students in Belfast, UK, unveiled a bridge made from some 11,000 pieces of Meccano on 1 Jul 2015. It spanned 28.76 m (94 ft 4 in) across the city's Clarendon Dock. Dr Danny McPolin, who led the project, said: "If you count all the nuts and bolts and washers, there's approximately 70,000 pieces." The bridge was opened by Meccano's very own Meccanoid robot (see right).

MEET MECCANOID

Its "Meccabrain" enables the Meccanoid G15KS to remember an hour's worth of voice commands.

The huge eyes were inspired by Pixar star WALL•E. They can also change between 500 different colours.

The robot is powered by a rechargeable 1,800 mAh battery.

Although this is the G15KS's default form, it can be reconfigured into any shape with additional Meccano parts.

The G15KS consists of 1,223 parts, made from polycarbonate rather than metal to keep the body light.

The robot moves on four wheels (two per foot), but can only travel in straight lines.

THE BIG PICTURE

In just two months, lifelong puzzler Tony Fisher (UK) built a supersized version of the classic toy with sides each measuring 1.57 m (5 ft 1.7 in). The **largest Rubik's Cube**, which resides in Ipswich, Suffolk, UK, was verified by Guinness World Records on 5 Apr 2016. It has already attracted the attention of puzzle fans, who have travelled from as far as Japan to see it.

"I am a Rubik's Cube fan and enjoy making and solving twisty puzzles in general. I am also fascinated by world records and have always wanted to set one." *Tony Fisher*

TOP TOYS

BLOCKBUSTER CHALLENGE
See pp.208-09

Even everyday playthings have inspired some breathtaking records. Join us now as we take a rummage through the GWR toy box...

MAGIC *Etch A Sketch* SCREEN

FASTEST 100 M ON A SPACEHOPPER
Boing! Serial record-breaker Ashrita Furman (USA, right) bounced his way to this record in just 30.2 sec in 2004.

MOST PEOPLE DRAWING ON AN ETCH A SKETCH
At an event organized by Jeff Gagliardi and Clark Hodge (both USA), 372 people of all ages put their artistic skills to the test on 25 Jun 2011. Each used an Etch A Sketch to draw a local mountain in Lyons, Colorado, USA.

LARGEST TOY PISTOL FIGHT
Jared's Epic NERF Battle, which took place at the AT&T Stadium in Arlington, Texas, USA, on 12 Mar 2016, saw 2,289 people wage war with the foam blasters.

MOST STAIRS DESCENDED BY A SLINKY
British scientists Marty Jopson (below left) and Hugh Hunt (below right) used their physics expertise to send a Slinky down 30 consecutive steps on an episode of *The One Show* in 2014.

It's widely believed that the word "yo-yo" comes from the Tagalog language of the Philippines: it means "return".

FASTEST TIME TO BUILD MR POTATO HEAD WHILE BLINDFOLDED

In 2012, Zoe Jayne Whalley (UK) pieced together Mr Potato Head in 16.17 sec in Gran Canaria, Spain – all without being able to see!

LARGEST YO-YO

Beth Johnson (USA) built a "Stars and Stripes" yo-yo with a diameter of 3.62 m (11 ft 10.5 in). To prove its "yo-yo-bility", it was dropped 36.5 m (120 ft) from a crane and successfully rebounded.

FIRST AI ROBOT TOY

The Furby was originally produced by Tiger Electronics (JPN) and took the form of a cuddly toy resembling Gizmo from the *Gremlins* movies. It first went on sale in 1998. Thanks to a series of built-in sensors, the cyber-pet could react to sound and motion, and it even spoke its own language called "Furbish".

LARGEST ROCKING HORSE

Gao Ming (CHN) built a 12.7-m-long (41-ft 8-in), 8.2-m-tall (26 ft 10.9 in) rocking horse that could carry 15 people at once. The pine-wood "rock star" was the *mane* attraction at a family arts festival themed around childhood that was held in Linyi, Shandong, China, in 2014.

FASTEST TIME TO SOLVE A RUBIK'S CUBE

Speed-cuber Lucas Etter (USA, below) became the first human to break the 5-sec barrier when he completed the classic puzzle in 4.90 sec on 21 Nov 2015. It's some way off the robot record, though (see p.163)...

MINECRAFT

When this open-world blockbuster arrived in 2009, who would have predicted the huge impact it would have on gaming and beyond?

BEST-SELLING PC GAME

Minecraft has now been ported to almost every platform imaginable, but it started out as a PC exclusive. As of 21 Jul 2016, the PC/Mac version of the game had shifted 23,922,451 copies, according to Mojang. In Jun 2016, Microsoft reported that *Minecraft* had sold in excess of 106 million copies across all platforms (mainly the *Pocket Edition*). In the first six months of 2016, an average 53,000 copies were sold per day.

CONFIDENTIAL

RUMOUR HAS IT...

In 2016, a release date for the official *Minecraft* movie was finally announced: 24 May 2019. Why such a long wait? Mojang said that it was "the right amount of time to make it completely awesome".

LONGEST MARATHON PLAYING *MINECRAFT*

Joseph Kelly (UK) spent 35 hr 35 min 35 sec in the virtual blocky world on 10–13 Oct 2015, mining to raise funds for Cancer Research UK.

MARVELLOUS MOBS   Meet some of *Minecraft*'s record-holding residents...

FIRST ANIMAL MOB

Pigs were the first creatures to roam the *Minecraft* world, appearing in the 0.24_05 release on 22 Aug 2009.

FIRST HOSTILE MOB

The first "enemies" were the zombies and skeletons that both arrived in the 0.24_02 release on 14 Aug 2009.

Using a name tag to retitle a mob "Dinnerbone" or "Grumm" – the nicknames of two *Minecraft* developers – results in flipping that character upside down.

MOST VIEWED FAN FILM BASED ON A GAME

A video created in *Minecraft* and uploaded to YouTube on 19 Aug 2011 by Jordan "CaptainSparklez" Maron (USA; see also p.62) had earned 163,883,566 views as of 21 Jul 2016. Originally titled "Revenge – A *Minecraft* Parody of Usher's DJ Got Us Fallin' in Love", its soundtrack was altered in 2016 and the video was renamed "Revenge – A *Minecraft* Original Music Video".

MOST REAL-WORLD THEME PARKS CREATED IN *MINECRAFT*

As of Jul 2016, the MCParks server hosted seven painstakingly rebuilt amusement parks, each at 1:1 scale. Virtual visitors can explore iconic real-life resorts such as Florida's Magic Kingdom and Universal Studios resorts (both pictured left).

9,776 km
Approximate distance that Kurt J Mac (below) had left to walk before he reached the Far Lands, as of Mar 2016.

LARGEST *MINECRAFT* PYRAMID

An international collaboration called The Stone Titans created a 1:1-scale replica of the Great Pyramid of Giza in Survival mode. Built from 2,629,176 blocks, it was verified in Toronto, Canada, on 2 Nov 2013. The mighty building includes all the passages, chambers and pits found in the real-life structure in Egypt – the world's **tallest pyramid**.

LONGEST JOURNEY IN *MINECRAFT*

In Mar 2011, Kurt J Mac (USA) set out on an epic quest to reach the fabled Far Lands in *Minecraft*. Kurt has been documenting the journey on his YouTube channel "Far Lands or Bust!". By 28 Mar 2016, his character had walked 2,723,612 blocks – that's the equivalent of 2,723.6 km (1,692.3 mi).

WEAKEST MOB

The chicken has only four Health Points (HP): two fewer than the bat, four fewer than the sheep and six fewer than the rabbit!

STRONGEST MOB

The Wither – a floating three-headed terror – has a mighty HP of 300, which is 100 points higher than its fellow boss mob, the Ender Dragon.

PEOPLE POWER: MINECRAFT STEVE

10,000
Tickets sold for the 2015 MineCon held in London, UK, making this the **largest convention dedicated to a single videogame.**

How cool would it be to play *Minecraft* at school? Well, students at Viktor Rydberg school in Sweden don't have to dream: compulsory *Minecraft* lessons were introduced there in 2013!

LARGEST GATHERING OF PEOPLE DRESSED AS MINECRAFT STEVE

As part of the MineVention conference held on 12 Sep 2015 in Peterborough, Cambridgeshire, UK, OBrien Event Management (IRL) rallied 337 *Minecraft* lovers to transform themselves into the sandbox game's iconic hero. Blockheads, assemble!

NEW KID ON THE BLOCKS

After four years being the only lead character in his blocky world, Steve was joined by a female counterpart in 2015, who goes by the name Alex (left). Initially an alternative skin that would randomly spawn in the Mac/PC versions, the character is now a selectable option across all ports of the blockbusting game. Mojang originally described *Minecraft*'s First Lady as having "thinner arms, redder hair and a ponytail". Some have said that she bears a passing resemblance to *Minecraft* programmer Jens Bergensten (above)... What do you think?!

CARD PLAY

Card games have been entertaining us for centuries, but today they come in more forms than ever before. Whether you're most *suit*ed to trading card games (TCGs), collectable card games (CCGs) or regular playing cards, there are records for all of them.

MOST PLAYED TRADING CARD GAME

First published by Wizards of the Coast (USA) in 1993, *Magic: The Gathering* has captured more people's imagination than any other TCG. As of 2015, it had cast a spell over an estimated audience of 20 million players worldwide including a committed following of professional players (see table). The enchanting franchise is also the **longest-running digital trading card game**, with computerized versions available since 1997.

HIGHEST TCG CAREER EARNINGS

Jon Finkel (USA, left)	$392,284 (£276,617)
Kai Budde (DEU)	$381,220 (£268,815)
Shuhei Nakamura (JPN)	$379,200 (£267,391)
Paulo Vitor Damo da Rosa (BRA)	$341,885 (£241,078)
Gabriel Nassif (FRA)	$341,710 (£240,995)

Source: magic.wizards.com; correct as of 29 Mar 2016

One of the earliest reports of a record-breaking card tower is a 15-storey structure credited to Victoria Maitland (UK) in *The Strand Magazine* in 1901.

LARGEST TRADING CARD

Most trading cards fit easily in the palm of your hand, but not this one... Produced by Panini America and revealed on 13 Feb 2010, the card depicts a life-size portrait of now-retired NBA basketball legend Kobe Bryant. Its dimensions are 2.13 x 1.49 m (7 ft x 4 ft 11 in).

LARGEST DECK OF PLAYING CARDS

Try giving these a shuffle! Made by Swedish schoolteacher Claes Blixt, the human-sized cards each measure 1.58 m tall by 1.04 m wide (5 ft 2.3 in x 3 ft 5.1 in), as confirmed on 14 May 2016.

It's not the first supersized record set by Claes: in 2013, he crafted the **longest table knife** – a 2.48-m-long (8-ft 1.6-in) wooden butter knife. As for his motives for living large, he said: "Big is always fun; everything that is big is fun."

MOST SUCCESSFUL *HEARTHSTONE* PLAYER

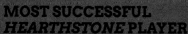

Since *Warcraft* spin-off *Hearthstone* launched in 2014, the online collectable card game has gone from strength to strength. As of 29 Apr 2016, no other player had earned more at dedicated tournaments of the turn-based title than James "Firebat" Kostesich (USA), with winnings of $218,428 (£151,601).

218,792
Cards used by Bryan Berg to recreate The Venetian Macao hotel resort in Macau, China. Standing 10.39 m (34 ft 1 in) tall, it was the **largest playing card structure.**

TALLEST HOUSE OF CARDS

Most of us can barely build a three-storey house of cards, but not *ace* card-stacker Bryan Berg (USA, right). In 2007 he constructed a soaring skyscraper out of 1,100 decks of cards, which reached a lofty 7.86 m (25 ft 9.7 in) high.

POKÉMON

Ash, Pikachu and co. just celebrated their 20th birthday, but they show no signs of retiring anytime soon. In fact, the franchise got a new lease of life with the runaway success of *Pokémon Go* in 2016. The question now is: what do the next 20 years have in store for the Pocket Monsters?

LARGEST COLLECTION OF POKÉMON MEMORABILIA

Mega Pokéfan Lisa Courtney (UK) hasn't caught them *all* yet, but she's way ahead of everyone else. As of 10 Aug 2016, she had 17,127 items, including cuddly toys, trading cards, badges, posters and clothing. Asked what's still on her wishlist, she told us: "I'm still searching for the Pokémon Center deluxe-size Tyranitar plush. I've been looking for him for over 10 years."

1,555
Items in the largest collection of *Lion King* memorabilia, as of 22 May 2015. Incredibly, this collection also belongs to Lisa Courtney (above)!

MOST POPULAR POKÉMON

1. GRENINJA
Types: Dark/Water
Pokédex: #658

2. ARCEUS
Type: Normal
Pokédex: #493

The name "Pikachu" combines the words for two sounds in Japanese: *pikapika* refers to the crackling of electricity, while *chuchu* is used to describe a squeaking noise.

LONGEST-RUNNING VIDEOGAME TV SPIN-OFF

The *Pokémon* anime series first screened on Japanese television back in 1997. In the franchise's 20th year, the show was on its 19th international season (based on the *XY* series, left). A total of 919 episodes had been aired as of 28 Apr 2016.

SMALLEST HAND-MADE POKÉMON SCULPTURES

Artist Ruby "Lonelysouthpaw" Huang (USA) builds tiny Pokémon characters out of clay. On average, they stand just 2–5 mm (0.07–0.19 in) tall. As of 5 Jan 2016, the smallest of them all was Voltorb (right), which measured a teeny 2 mm (0.07 in) in all dimensions.

LEAST POPULAR POKÉMON

Of the 562,386 Trainers and fans polled in the 2016 Pokémon General Election, candy-loving Fire-type Simisear came 720th out of 720. For the most popular, see the bar below.

FASTEST MOBILE GAME TO GROSS $100 M

Within its debut month, *Pokémon Go* reached this milestone in a Deoxys-quick 20 days, after its US launch on 6 Jul 2016. This game-changing app combines the much-loved characters with the real world (left) via augmented-reality (AR) tech. Now, wherever you go, your smartphone or tablet acts as your very own Pokédex, enabling you to capture any Pocket Monsters you encounter. The creatures are typically found in the habitats most suited to their type. For instance, to catch a Poliwag you would need to head towards water in the game's GPS view (inset).

 3. MEW
Type: Psychic
Pokédex: #151

4. PIKACHU
Type: Electric
Pokédex: #25

5. SYLVEON
Type: Fairy
Pokédex: #700

Source: Pokémon General Election, 2016

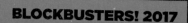

MODEL CARS

When it comes to toy cars, the race is always on to be the first across the finish line. But how they get there depends entirely on the record...

MOST EXPENSIVE TOY CAR

A red and green "Dinky" delivery van fetched £19,975 ($39,801) at an online auction by Vectis in 2008. The Hornby toy was originally made in the mid-1930s. Its rarest feature is the logo on its side: W E Boyce was the name of an early 20th-century bicycle shop in London, UK.

LARGEST COLLECTION OF MODEL CARS

Rally driver Nabil "Billy" Karam (LBN) owned a staggering 37,777 toy cars as of 9 Jun 2016. This avid collector also owns the **largest collection of dioramas** (example inset right), with 577 as of the same date. Dioramas are detailed 3D model sets that recreate real-life scenes in miniature.

The mega-collections are exhibited in a warehouse in Lebanon, owned by the Karam family. Although the museum is private, it is often opened for public viewings; around 25,000 visitors are estimated to have seen the record-breaking displays.

HOT WHEELS HISTORY   Our top picks from the last five decades of Hot Wheels

1968
Custom Mustang
Designer:
Harry Bradley

1978
'57 T-Bird
Designers:
Larry Wood/Bob Rosas

1988
Nissan Hardbody
Designer:
Larry Wood

Hot Wheels isn't all about cars. In 2016, the company produced a special-edition "Yellow Submarine" in honour of the Beatles song released 50 years before.

LARGEST MODEL VEHICLE BRAND (CURRENT, RETAIL)

In terms of retail sales, Mattel's Hot Wheels (USA) is in pole position. In 2015, the range raced away with approximately $866.2 m (£584.2 m) worth of sales, according to Euromonitor International as of 1 Jun 2016.

LARGEST HOT WHEELS LOOP

Matt and Blade West, John Jaranson, Grant Compton, Jeff Schoppert, James Barnabei, John Gambino and Tim Walker (all USA) built a loop with a diameter of 3.81 m (12 ft 6 in) in Dearborn, Michigan, USA. The team's effort was part of Ford's "bring your child to work day" on 5 May 2015.

MATCHBOX vs HOT WHEELS

MATCHBOX

Introduced: 1953	Standard scale: 1:64
Manufactured by: Mattel (USA)	Key themes: sport, monster trucks, space, sci-fi

Hot Wheels

Introduced: 1968	Standard scale: 1:64
Manufactured by: Mattel (USA)	Key themes: sport, military, construction

LARGEST TOY CAR MOSAIC

Mini China used 1,034 mini Mini cars to create a 10.767-m² (115.89-sq-ft) mosaic in Guangzhou, Guangdong, China, on 15 Jun 2013. The final work depicted the Union Jack (left), flag of the United Kingdom, from where the iconic car originates.

1998
At-A-Tude
Designer: Mark Jones

2008
H₂Go
Designer: Larry Wood

2016
Night Shifter
Designer: Larry Wood

THE BIG PICTURE

"The speed is critical. I need to make sure I hit the magic number to drive through the loop [or] it's not going to be possible. I had to concentrate on that and just calm myself down." *Terry Grant*

Ever imagined how it would feel to be at the controls of a Hot Wheels car? Stunt driver Terry Grant (UK) found out exactly what it's like on 14 Sep 2015. At the wheel of a Jaguar F-PACE during the car's public launch in Frankfurt, Germany, he completed a dizzying loop that stood 19.08 m (62 ft 7 in) off the ground. It was the **largest loop-the-loop in a car**.

CONSOLE GAMING

The eighth generation of consoles is now well underway, with the PlayStation 4 leading the pack, but rumours of imminent hardware updates mean that the field is still wide open. Here we look at a few of the big titles that had console gamers hooked in recent months.

HIGHEST SCORE ON *GUITAR HERO LIVE*

"Lo11o2" scored 663,622 playing the Expert-level guitar part of "I Will Wait" by Mumford & Sons, in a video uploaded to YouTube on 11 Jan 2016. Lo11o2 strummed more than 1,000 correct notes in a row playing the catchy country-rock number.

FASTEST COMPLETION OF *RATCHET & CLANK* (2016)

Just eight days after its North American release on 12 Apr 2016, US Twitcher "Raikaru" finished the remake of the sci-fi platformer in 1 hr 16 min 45 sec. His run relied on the "Bouncer" – a pre-order weapon for the game.

31
Number of hi-tech weapons and crazy gadgets featured in 2016's *Ratchet & Clank.* Across the entire series, there have been more than 200 weapons.

In the original 2002 version of the game, Clank started on the side of Ratchet's enemy, Chairman Drek. On hearing of his master's evil plans, though, the robot changed his allegiance.

MOST OPPONENTS IN *STREET FIGHTER V*

Pro eSports athlete Ryan Hart (UK) went up against 260 consecutive challengers during an 11-hr *Street Fighter V* marathon in Manchester, UK, on 16 Feb 2016. He was required to win 90% of the matches to earn the record, but he managed to KO *every* competitor, achieving a 100% success rate.

FASTEST COMPLETION OF *STAR FOX ZERO*

On 2 May 2016, US gamer "Rodriguezjr" finished Fox McCloud's Wii U space actioner in 36 min 29 sec (in-game time 27 min 48 sec), as verified by Speedrun.com. The run was completed in Arcade mode.

Q&A WITH... STEVE BLUM

GWR caught up with the most prolific videogame voice actor, who had appeared in 357 games as of Mar 2016.

Q **How do you get into a new character?**

A I didn't have a classical acting education, so I work mostly by intuition. I find the best way for me to approach any new character is exactly the same way I used to play with toys as a child. I see a drawing or model of a character, or am given a description, and I let the imagination take over. I try not to second-guess it, I just dive in and deliver as organically as possible.

Q **What have you been working on recently?**

A *Mighty No.9* – the little game that could! It's a crowdfunded action platformer inspired by classics like *Mega Man*. Its release was delayed a few times, but I have a feeling it was worth the wait.

Q **Hero or villain: which is better to play?**

A I began my career playing villains and spent years honing my bad-boy growls, howls and roars. It's tremendously fun and therapeutic, but it can be painful. The satisfaction I get from playing heroes is simpler. Their motives are clear and children don't fear me. Heroes with an edge, like X-Men's Wolverine, are the most interesting.

MOBILE GAMING

For better or worse, the days of *Snake* and *Tetris* are long behind us. But while ever-more-complex gaming apps come to our pocket devices, it's often the simplest ones that command the biggest audiences...

862

The **highest score on *Crossy Road*** (see opposite), set on 12 Jun 2016. It was achieved by Ronnie Weston (UK) on an iPad, while raising money for charity Parkinson's UK.

MOST PLAYED MOBILE VIDEOGAME (CURRENT)

According to SuperData, *Candy Crush Saga* (2012, left) was the most played mobile gaming app in 2015. King's colourful puzzle game enjoyed an average 182,892,377 monthly active users (MAU) across the year. It was also 2015's **most played free2play game**, with an MAU count of 261,534,233 across both social media and mobile platforms.

MOST WATCHED VIDEOGAME TV ADVERT

The *Clash of Clans: Revenge* official Super Bowl TV ad had been viewed 128,743,159 times on YouTube as of 2 Sep 2016. The commercial made its debut during half-time at Super Bowl XLIX in 2015. It features a chilling "AngryNeeson52", aka Hollywood actor Liam Neeson (inset below).

MOST POPULAR ZOMBIE IN *PLANTS VS. ZOMBIES: GARDEN WARFARE*

As of Nov 2015, more than 1.4 billion games of *Plants vs. Zombies: Garden Warfare* (2014) had been played. Of these, the class of zombie most often chosen was Foot Soldier (right), with a total of 545 million spawns. The **most popular plant**, meanwhile, was the Peashooter (left), with 534 million spawns.

Q&A WITH... HIPSTER WHALE

We caught up with Matt Hall (far right) of Australian indie app developer Hipster Whale. Along with fellow co-founder Andy Sum (near right), they are the creative minds behind the smash-hit mobile game *Crossy Road*.

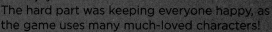

Q **Which was the first mobile game you became addicted to playing? Are there any you're hooked on right now?**

A *Flight Control* was the first game that really showed how great touch-screen games could be. *Steppy Pants* is the game we've all been playing lately!

Q **Why do you think that *Crossy Road* has proven so popular?**

A *Crossy Road* is a mix of *Flappy Bird*, *Frogger* and *Skylanders*. I loved collecting *Skylanders* with my daughter and I hoped that people would love collecting our figurines in the same way.

Q **Tell us about the making of *Disney Crossy Road* (left).**

A *Crossy Road* was made very quickly, in just 12 weeks.

Disney Crossy Road took 12 months. Giving each of the worlds different "rules" was the part we enjoyed the most. The hard part was keeping everyone happy, as the game uses many much-loved characters!

Q **What's your favourite Disney movie of all time and why?**

A That's a very tough question. I think that *WALL·E* is probably my favourite, but *Wreck-It Ralph* is a very close second. I love the way that the director joined all the videogame worlds together.

Q **What's on the horizon for Hipster Whale?**

A *Disney Crossy Road* will keep us busy for some time as there are more worlds to add. But Andy and I have more ideas we want to make...

Q **Finally, hit us with your best "Why did the chicken cross the road?" joke.**

A Why did the duck cross the road? To prove he wasn't chicken.

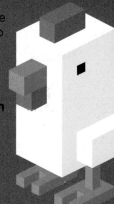

HIGHEST MATCHING SCORE ON *FRUIT NINJA* IN ONE MINUTE (TEAM OF TWO)

Mohammed Mahamroot (UK, far left holding certificate) and Ryan Lobo (IND, left holding certificate) took on this team challenge at Legends of Gaming held in London, UK, on 11 Sep 2016. In 60 sec, they each sliced 130 points of fruit, working together to ensure their scores tallied exactly.

PC GAMING

PC games are known for packing a punch when it comes to graphics and scale, bringing global communities together in epic virtual worlds.

MOST PLAYED ONLINE MULTIPLAYER GAME (CURRENT)

According to SuperData, the battle arena game *League of Legends* (*LoL*) had an average of 94,332,069 monthly active users throughout 2015. *LoL* has become one of the most popular eSports titles (see pp.158–59). As of 17 Aug 2016, $29,508,613 (£22.7 m) of prize money had been awarded in *LoL* tournaments.

WOW!

TOP 5 PC SIMULATION GAMES

TITLE	RATING
The Sims 2 (2004, right)	90.76%
The Sims (2000)	89.74%
Silent Hunter III (2005)	88.65%
Steel Beasts (2000)	87.58%
Microsoft Flight Simulator 2004: A Century of Flight (2003)	87.07%

Source: GameRankings.com; correct as of 15 Aug 2016

In Sep 2005, a deadly virtual plague, dubbed "Corrupted Blood", broke out in *World of Warcraft*, affecting thousands of players. It is regarded as the **first videogame pandemic**.

MOST EXPLORABLE PLANETS IN A VIDEOGAME

Space-based adventure game *No Man's Sky* (2016) is perfect for explorers. The elements it mixes to create planets can be combined in 18.4 quintillion different ways. This means that the game has twice as many unique planets as there are grains of sand on Earth, and each can be landed on and explored!

585 bn
Estimated number of years it would take to visit each of the worlds in *No Man's Sky* – and that's at a rate of finding a planet every second!

LONGEST *WORLD OF WARCRAFT* MARATHON

Spanish gamer Hecaterina Kinumi Iglesias (aka Kinumi Cati, left) played Blizzard's classic RPG *World of Warcraft* in Vigo, Spain, for 29 hr 31 min on 29–30 Mar 2014. The avid cosplayer also set the **longest *Final Fantasy* marathon**, playing for 38 hr 6 min in 2013.

MOST CROWDFUNDED VIDEOGAME

By 12 Feb 2016, the space-faring simulator *Star Citizen* – designed by *Wing Commander* creator Chris Roberts (USA) – had raised an out-of-this-world $108,028,009 (£74.5 m) from 1.2 million Kickstarter backers. This makes it not only the most crowdfunded videogame, but also the **most crowdfunded project** overall.

eSPORTS

What was once just a chance to earn bragging rights over your mates has now become an opportunity to achieve global fame and mega-bucks...

$241.6 bn
Total prize money awarded since records began, as of 15 Aug 2016. The prizes were paid out across 17,984 eSports contests.

LARGEST PRIZE POOL FOR AN eSPORTS TOURNAMENT

Smashing its own previous year's record, the International 2016 global *Dota 2* championship (above), which took place on 8–13 Aug 2016 in Seattle, Washington, USA, raised an epic $20,770,460 (£16 m) in prize money. The winners of the contest, Chinese eSports team Wings Gaming (below), took home the lion's share – $9,139,002 (£7 m) – which is the **largest first prize in an eSports competition**.

TOP 5 eSPORTS EARNERS

Peter "ppd" Dager (USA, right)	$2,617,389 (£2.02 m)
Saahil "UNiVeRsE" Arora (USA)	$2,606,414 (£2.01 m)
Clinton "Fear" Loomis (USA)	$2,382,424 (£1.84 m)
Sumail "Suma1L" Hassan (PAK)	$2,287,216 (£1.76 m)
Li "iceice" Peng (CHN)	$1,932,462 (£1.49 m)

Source: e-Sports Earnings; correct as of 15 Aug 2016

In May 2016, West Ham United became the first British football club to sign an eSports player: Sean Allen (aka "Dragonn"). The gamer was runner-up in 2016's *FIFA* Interactive World Cup.

MOST eSPORTS TOURNAMENTS FOR A VIDEOGAME

As of 29 Jun 2016, *StarCraft II: Wings of Liberty* (2010) had provided the battleground for 3,688 eSports tournaments. According to e-Sports Earnings, 1,539 players had collectively won $19,349,087 (£14.4 m) from the title, making the real-time strategy the third most lucrative eSports game only behind *Dota 2* and *League of Legends* (*LoL*).

FIRST PROFESSIONAL SPORTS CLUB TO ACQUIRE AN eSPORTS TEAM

On 20 Jan 2015, Beşiktaş Istanbul – owner of Turkey's Beşiktaş JK soccer team – acquired the *League of Legends* side Aces High. Although their contract was not renewed a year later, it kicked off a new trend. German soccer club FC Schalke bought the *LoL* team Elements in 2016,

Q&A WITH... "SUMA1L"

We caught up with Sumail "Suma1L" Hassan, who aged 16 years 82 days became the youngest eSports gamer to earn $1 million.

Q How does it feel to be a role model for legions of gamers around the world?

A Winning the world championships [in 2015] was what mattered. I got to prove that I am the best. The money was just a bonus. I got to buy my family a house.

Q Tell us how you first got into gaming.

A I got into gaming when I was around seven years old. The first game I played was *Age of Empires*. I have only played three computer games in my life: *Counter-Strike*, *Age of Empires* and *Dota 2* [left].

Q What do you think makes a successful *Dota 2* player?

A Hard work, dedication, teamwork, winning tournaments and, my personal favourite, skills.

Q How much training do you have to do?

A Every single player in my team [Evil Geniuses, who won the International 2015] plays for about 10 hr a day. It really depends on how much you want to improve. If you want to become the best, you just keep playing.

Q Finally, any tips for aspiring eSports stars?

A If you want to be something, you have to give it your all and give up every other thing to achieve the dream.

VIRTUAL REALITY

With the rise of VR technology, the lines between imaginary and real have never been more blurred.

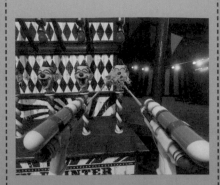

LONGEST VR APP MARATHON

Derek Westerman (USA) spent 25 hr 2 min painting in the art app *Tilt Brush* in Los Angeles, California, USA, on 6–7 Apr 2016. He was playing on an HTC Vive.

ALL THE FUN OF THE VR FAIR...

Technology firm NVIDIA has always been focused on the hardware side of computing, but now it is branching out into software too. *VR Funhouse*, which launched in Jul 2016, is the company's very first videogame. Compatible with the HTC Vive headset, the title takes gamers on a colourful trip to the carnival. Mini-games revolve around traditional fairground attractions, such as whacking moles, smashing crockery and a number of shooting galleries.

LARGEST AR/VR HEADSET BRAND

Based on Euromonitor International data retrieved on 16 Jun 2016, Samsung's (KOR) Gear VR had estimated sales of $43,041,400 (£30.3 m) in 2015. The device works with the S6 phone or Galaxy Note5 to make watching videos and gaming far more immersive.

MOST EXPENSIVE VR ACQUISITION

When Facebook bought Oculus Rift in 2014, it paid $400 m (£242.5 m) in cash, supplemented by 23.1 million Facebook shares – then worth $1.6 bn (£970.2 m). It also added $300 m (£181.9 m) in incentives based on targets being met. This easily makes it the priciest purchase of any VR company to date.

At Star Wars Celebration Europe 2016, Lucasfilm announced that it is in the early stages of developing a VR short film about Darth Vader in which viewers will become "part of the story".

FIRST VR "FLYING" ROLLER-COASTER

Opened on 24 Mar 2016, Galactica at Alton Towers in Staffordshire, UK, is the first ride of its type to incorporate virtual-reality tech. On a flying roller-coaster, the cars hang below the tracks rather than sitting on top, creating a sensation of flight. Each seat is fitted with a Gear VR that transports the wearer into space. What riders view via the headsets is synced to the dips and curves of the track, simulating a voyage through the cosmos, with planets and other spacecraft to dodge on the way.

3.5 g
Top g-force experienced on Galactica. The ride started out as another roller-coaster called Air, which opened back in 2002.

ASTRONAUT'S SEAL OF APPROVAL

Canadian astronaut Chris Hadfield (centre right), who recorded the **first music video in space** in 2013, was Galactica's very first rider when it launched. Afterwards, he told the press: "This is one of the best rides I've ever been on and I've been on some rides. I've been lucky enough to serve on three space flights, including five months on the *International Space Station*, but this is as close as I've come to a virtual trip across the universe."

ROBOTOYS & DRONES

Just as so many sci-fi movies predicted, robots are increasingly becoming part of our everyday lives... Putting their serious applications aside for a moment, here we prove that they know how to have fun too!

MOST ROBOTS DANCING SIMULTANEOUSLY

Almost doubling the previous record, Ever Win Company & Ltd (CHN) got 1,007 robots boogying in Qingdao, Shandong, China, on 30 Jul 2016. Incredibly, all of the droids were controlled by a single smartphone. A few were disqualified as they fell over or didn't move, but the majority of the mechanical dance troupe completed the 60-sec routine in perfect unison.

WOW!

FASTEST FIVE-CONE SLALOM BY A SPHERICAL ROBOT

With Richard Beckett (UK, right) at the controls, BB-8 slalomed around five cones and back in a speedy 15.26 sec at the Gadget Show Live held in Birmingham, UK, on 1 Apr 2016. Many visitors took on the challenge at the GWR Live! event, but Richard topped the leaderboard.

In 2016, the British TV series *Robot Wars* made its return, 13 years after it last aired. The show revolves around inventors building battle-bots that fight for supremacy in a special arena.

FASTEST ROBOT TO SOLVE A RUBIK'S CUBE

This hotly contested record has exchanged robotic hands four times since 2014. The current holder, Sub1, solved the classic puzzle in a blistering 0.887 sec in Munich, Germany, on 23 Jan 2016. It was built by Albert Beer (DEU).

HIGHEST ALTITUDE FOOTBALL DROPPED AND CONTROLLED

Football freestyler John Farnworth (UK, above) controlled a ball released by a modified drone hovering 32 m (104 ft 11.8 in) overhead. The record took place at Harlow Town Football Club in Essex, UK, on 23 May 2016.

THE BIG PICTURE

Hoping to stop people picking on him during NERF battles at work, former NASA engineer Mark Rober (USA) built the **largest NERF gun**, assisted by Ryan and David, hosts of the science YouTube channel Eclectical Engineering. The supersized blaster measures 6 ft (1.82 m) long, as verified by Guinness World Records on 22 Jun 2016. The air-powered projectiles – which at 24 in (61 cm) are almost nine times the length of standard NERF bullets – leave the barrel at roughly 40 mph (64 km/h)!

"Friends and family are no longer impressed when I make a YouTube video that gets millions of views, but I got quite a few high fives when I told them about earning a GWR title." *Mark Rober*

TOP 10: ACTION FIGURES

Since the arrival in 1964 of the **first action figure**, G.I. Joe (aka Action Man in the UK), no self-respecting toy box has been complete without one or two of these poseable models. These days, the most popular plastic players are nearly all scaled-down versions of heroes associated with both the big and small screens, although the most successful of them all – based on the latest sales figures from 2015 – is an exception...

PLAYMOBIL **1**
Geobra Brandstätter GmbH & Co (DEU)
$654,827,000 (£450.7 m)

Playmobil was the brainchild of German inventor Hans Beck. He wanted to strike the perfect balance between flexibility and rigidity in his figurines and to create a toy that would fit the size of the average child's hand. Nowadays they come in dozens of different "themes", including Egyptians, Knights and Pirates (left), along with a wide range of extras, such as buildings, vehicles and other accessories.

STAR WARS **2**
Hasbro Inc (USA)
$600,254,700 (£413.2 m)

Rebooting a toy line that had been discontinued in the 1980s, Hasbro introduced a new *Star Wars* series in 1995 and hasn't looked back since. *The Force Awakens*, 2015's top-grossing movie, also sparked some of the year's most sought-after toys, such as BB-8 (left). In terms of merchandise, the movie is estimated to have hauled in $5 bn (£3.3 bn), adding to the franchise's record total.

TEENAGE MUTANT NINJA TURTLES **3**
Playmates Toys Ltd (USA)
$346,640,000 (£238.6 m)

Raphael, Donatello, Leonardo (above) and Michelangelo made their debut in comic books in the mid-1980s before moving to TV and finally the big screen. Their latest cinema outing, *TMNT: Out of the Shadows*, hit movie theatres in Jun 2016 and no doubt had fans *shelling* out for a whole new range of tie-in toys.

TRANSFORMERS **4**
Hasbro Inc
$325,141,800 (£223.8 m)

In toy shops, Hasbro's "Robots in Disguise" are anything but discreet. They are rare in that they arrived as action figures *before* they appeared in the movies. And what a lucrative acting career they have had. The five *Transformers* films to date have taken $3,778,297,170 (£2.42 bn) – the **highest-grossing movie series based on a toy franchise**.

Which of the top 10 best-selling toy brands have been on sale the longest as of 2017?

1975
Playmobil
(42 years)

1978
Star Wars
(39 years)

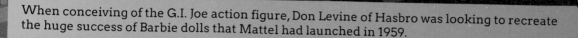

When conceiving of the G.I. Joe action figure, Don Levine of Hasbro was looking to recreate the huge success of Barbie dolls that Mattel had launched in 1959.

WWE 5
Mattel Inc (USA)
$177,025,700 (£121.8 m)

When it comes to wrestling franchises, WWE easily KOs the competition. Although Mattel only took over the line in 2010, WWE toys date back to 1984 (see timeline below). In addition to the articulated models of famous fighters such as Triple H and John Cena (left), the range also includes arenas and dress-up items, such as masks and wrestling belts.

POWER RANGERS 6
Bandai Namco Group (USA)
$154,069,500 (£106.0 m)

Inspired by Japan's *Super Sentai* series, the Power Rangers have been battling baddies bent on world domination, as well as oversized monsters, since 1993. Each character's unique abilities and weapons made them prime candidates for action-toy makeovers. A third feature movie is slated for 2017.

MAX STEEL
Mattel Inc $102,987,400 (£70.8 m)

The Max Steel franchise underwent a "Turbo"-powered revamp after its debut TV spin-off in 2000. The hero has since diversified into several sub-lines, with figures including everything from Vertical Lift Off Max to Ninja Max. The high-action secret agent is one of Mattel's biggest-selling toys in Latin America.

7

AVENGERS
Hasbro Inc
$90,552,000 (£62.3 m)

Toy sales of Thor, Captain America, the Hulk and other Avengers rocketed in 2015 off the back of the second movie, *Age of Ultron* (released in May 2015). One of the most popular new figures to hit the shelves was the Hulkbuster Iron Man (pictured; be sure to check out the life-size one on p.170). The Avengers range also features masks, accessories, vehicles and weapons.

8

ARMOR HERO 9
Guangdong Alpha Animation & Culture Co (CHN)
$86,968,800 (£59.8 m)

The story of this Chinese mega-brand revolves around young heroes who are able to summon elemental forces – and super-cool suits – in order to fight evil. In 2015, Hasbro revealed that it was working on Armor Hero sets for its growing Kre-O construction toy range.

MARVEL 10
Hasbro Inc
$72,933,700 (£50.2 m)

The Avengers (see No.8) are not the only stars of the Marvel toy empire manufactured by Hasbro. Other famous lines include Spider-Man, Guardians of the Galaxy and X-Men, as well as the ever-growing Super Hero Masher series, which lets you mix and match characters (such as the War Machine figure, right).

Source: Euromonitor International, 2015 retail sales data; figures retrieved on 8 Jun 2016

1984
Transformers (33 years)

1984
WWE (33 years)

1987
Teenage Mutant Ninja Turtles (30 years)

WINNING FORMULA

While riding on the Formula Rossa roller-coaster in Abu Dhabi, UAE, you'll experience a force of 4.8 g; by contrast, an astronaut only experiences around 3 g during a rocket launch!

Having a whale of a time...

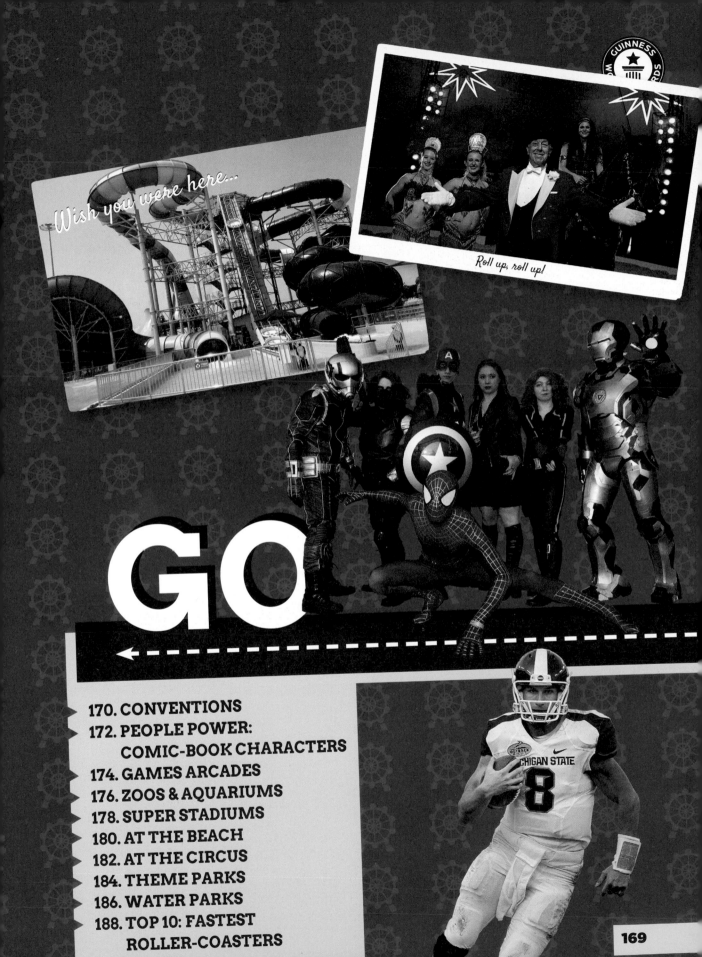

Wish you were here...

Roll up, roll up!

GO

CONVENTIONS

Providing a place for like-minded fans to dress up, come together and meet a few of their heroes (real and fictional), these mega-events have now gone mainstream. Today, they are attracting bigger crowds than ever before...

1,600
Hours that DePetrillo put into building the Hulkbuster over a period of two years. It takes around 20 min for him to get into the costume.

LARGEST COSPLAY COSTUME (SINGLE PERSON)

The Iron Man Hulkbuster, designed and built by cosplayer Thomas DePetrillo (USA) of Extreme Costumes, is the largest one-person cosplay outfit that is fully mobile. The suit stands 9 ft 6 in (2.89 m) tall and has a shoulder width of 6 ft 4 in (1.93 m). It weighs in at 106 lb (48 kg). The colossal costume was first unveiled at New York Comic Con in Oct 2015.

LARGEST GAMES CONVENTION

Gamescom 2016 (above), held at the Koelnmesse in Cologne, Germany, on 17–21 Aug welcomed 345,000 visitors from 97 countries, matching 2015's attendance. The event featured stands from 877 different gaming companies. Among the attendees was *GWR Gamer's* Editor Stephen Daultrey, whose highlight was getting the chance to see through the eyes of Batman in the new VR version of *Batman Arkham*.

LONGEST-RUNNING TRANSFORMERS CONVENTION

BotCon has been held every year since 1994, when the first show attracted about 150 attendees. It has since grown into a four-day event, endorsed by Hasbro, with thousands of visitors.

LARGEST COMIC-BOOK FESTIVAL

No event attracts more fans of comic books – or manga, as they're called in Japan – than Comiket (short for "Comic Market"), which is held twice a year at the Big Sight convention centre in Tokyo, Japan. The 2016 summer festival attracted 530,000 people. Amazingly, this is not its all-time record. Comiket 84 (inset right), held in Aug 2013, received 590,000 manga-lovers over three days.

GWR DOES COMIC CON

GWR adjudicator Vicky Tweedy (far left) attended 2016's London Comic Con. What did she think? "The first thing you notice are all the cosplayers. There was someone in a lit-up War Machine costume from *Iron Man 3* and a guy in a huge Baymax suit. As well as walking the floor, I got to meet some amazing record holders, such as former *Doctor Who* star Peter Davison [near left]."

PEOPLE POWER: COMIC-BOOK CHARACTERS

LARGEST GATHERING OF PEOPLE DRESSED AS COMIC-BOOK CHARACTERS

A record-breaking 1,784 comic-book fans dressed up as their favourite superheroes and villains at the Salt Lake Comic Con, held in Salt Lake City, Utah, USA, on 25 Sep 2015. Guinness World Records adjudicator Michael Empric attended the event to greet and count the characters as they entered the arena.

A last-minute call for attendees in comic-book costumes was put out at Salt Lake Comic Con 2015 to make sure they hit the record. As you can see below, it paid off!

120,000
Total attendance at the 2015 Salt Lake Comic Con – the same number as 2014 and about 50,000 more than the inaugural event, which took place in 2013.

GAMES ARCADES

With all the ever-smarter devices that fit in our pockets satisfying our gaming fix, it's easy to forget where the videogames revolution began.

35,000
Estimated sales of *Pong* machines, making the Atari trendsetter the first commercially successful arcade videogame.

MOST PEOPLE PLAYING PINBALL SIMULTANEOUSLY

A total of 331 retro gaming fans played pinball together on 17 Jan 2015. The record attempt took place as part of the inaugural Arcade Expo, held at the Museum of Pinball in Banning, California, USA.

LARGEST VIDEOGAME ARCADE

As of 12 Jan 2016, Funspot at Weirs Beach in New Hampshire, USA, was home to 581 games across three floors. Founded in 1952 by Bob Lawton, the venue's American Classic Arcade Museum alone has over 250 working machines from the 1970s and 1980s.

LARGEST HUMAN IMAGE OF PAC-MAN

Sony Pictures Entertainment Japan recruited 351 employees to recreate arcade gaming's most iconic character in front of the Tokyo Tower in Japan on 21 May 2015. As well as celebrating *PAC-Man*'s 35th birthday, the event was also organized to promote the release of the movie *Pixels* (below).

OLD-SCHOOL ARCADES

Even before the early games such as *Pong* and *Space Invaders*, there were arcades. Their star attractions included slot machines, self-playing instruments and other forms of mechanical entertainment, such as fortune-tellers and tests of strength. One of the best-known antique arcades still open is the Musée Mécanique on San Francisco's waterfront in California, USA. There, you'll find 300 vintage exhibits, including the creepy "Laffing Sal" (right).

SMALLEST vs LARGEST ARCADE MACHINE

The mini "Markade" was built by Canadian computer engineer Mark Slevinsky. Its diminutive dimensions are 124 x 52 x 60 mm (4.88 x 2.05 x 2.36 in). Its retro offerings include *Tetris*, *Breakout* and *Space Invaders*.

This mega-machine stands 4.41 m (14 ft 5.6 in) tall, as verified on 23 Mar 2015. It was made by network engineer Jason Camberis (USA). The 250-plus pre-installed games include classics such as *Dragon Spirit* and *PAC-Man*.

1 x **largest arcade machine** = 35.5 x **smallest arcade machine**

ZOOS & AQUARIUMS

Whether you're a fan of fur or scales, wildlife parks and aquariums make for some of the most popular attractions on the planet. It must be the animal magnetism!

MOST ZOOS VISITED

Between 1987 and 2014, wildlife fan Jonas Livet (FRA) travelled to 873 zoos in 47 countries. He is shown below at two of the zoos: one in Chinese Taipei (left) and one in the USA (right).

LARGEST AQUARIUM

The Hengqin Ocean Kingdom – part of the wider Chimelong resort owned by Zhuhai Chimelong Investment and Development Co., Ltd (CHN) – has a total volume of 48.75 million litres (12.87 million US gal) of both fresh and salt water. The Chinese park is also home to the **largest aquarium tank** (above) and the **largest underwater viewing dome** (rendered image bottom right), both of which are part of the whale shark exhibit.

The term "aquarium" was coined in 1894 by English naturalist Philip Henry Gosse to describe what was then called the "Fish House" at London Zoo in the UK.

OLDEST CONTINUOUSLY OPERATING ZOO

The Tiergarten Schönbrunn in Vienna, Austria, was created in 1752 as a royal menagerie, by order of Holy Roman Emperor Francis I. It was first opened to the public in 1779 and remains a popular attraction to this day.

TALLEST CYLINDRICAL AQUARIUM

Shoppers at the Aviapark Mall in Moscow, Russia, can enjoy some 2,500 fish that live in its 20.31-m-tall (66-ft 7.6-in) aquarium. The tank is so big that, when divers venture to the bottom, they must make multiple decompression stops during their ascent. The three-storey aquarium was officially measured on 28 Oct 2015.

LARGEST REPTILE ZOO

Reptile Gardens, near Rapid City in South Dakota, USA, was home to more than 225 different reptiles as of 2013. Record-breaking residents include the **largest venomous lizard**, the Komodo dragon (right), and the West African gaboon viper, which boasts the **longest fangs on a snake**.

80
Years since Reptile Gardens was founded by Earl Brockelsby. He is famous for keeping a rattlesnake under his hat while giving guided tours!

SUPER STADIUMS

Playing host to blockbuster sports events and superlative athletes, these mega feats of architecture are raising the roof to break records of their own. To give some context of just how massive they are, we have included the entire national population(s) that each could hold...

LARGEST SOLAR-POWERED STADIUM

The green credentials of the National Stadium in Kaohsiung, Chinese Taipei, are second to none, with 8,844 solar panels producing 80% of the building's power. Designed by Japanese architect Toyo Ito for the 2009 World Games, the eco-stadium can hold 55,000 spectators.

POPULATION
AMERICAN SAMOA: 54,343

LARGEST FOOTBALL STADIUM

Home of the Wolverines, the Michigan Stadium in Ann Arbor, Michigan, USA, has 109,901 seats – enough to fit Tonga's population of 106,501, with 3,400 spaces to spare! The arena also held the **largest ice hockey match audience**, when 104,173 people watched the University of Michigan and Michigan State University face off on the frozen field (above) on 11 Dec 2010.

POPULATION
TONGA: 106,501

WOW!

660
Tonnes of carbon dioxide produced by traditional power stations being saved by the solar panels on Taipei's National Stadium each year.

Football fan Alicia Barnhart (USA) watched games at all 31 NFL stadiums in just 86 days 10 hr 25 min in 2015 – the **fastest time to visit all NFL stadiums**.

LARGEST SUMO STADIUM

Located in Tokyo, Japan, Ryōgoku Kokugikan can hold 11,908 sumo fans – though probably nowhere near that if filled with sumo wrestlers! The ringside seats, known as the *suna-aburi-seki*, are so close to the action that spectators are often showered with sand during bouts!

POPULATION
TUVALU: 10,869

CONFIDENTIAL

RUMOUR HAS IT...

One of several new arenas proposed for the 2022 FIFA World Cup in Qatar is the Doha Port Stadium (below). It will sit on a man-made strip of land, jutting into the city's harbour. The players better pack their swim-suits!

LARGEST STADIUM

No other venue can beat the Indianapolis Motor Speedway in Indiana, USA, in terms of capacity, with seating for up to 257,325 motorheads. Home to the famous "Indy 500" and "Brickyard 400" races, the speedway was built in 1909 and contains a 4.09-km (2.5-mi) oval circuit, among other tracks.

POPULATION
SEYCHELLES: 92,430

+

POPULATION
ST LUCIA: 163,922

Population totals from CIA, correct as of Jul 2015

AT THE BEACH

Oh we do like to be beside the seaside... and why not, with such a wide range of record-breaking opportunities on offer? Come on a journey to the beach with us as we celebrate everything sand, sea, surf – and supersized...

TALLEST SANDCASTLE

Standing the same height as three stacked double-decker buses, Ted Siebert (USA) of the Sand Sculpture Company led a team of 19 to build a 13.97-m-high (45-ft 10-in) sandcastle, as verified on 27 Oct 2015. The multi-tiered construction (see inset) was sculpted on Virginia Key Beach in Miami, Florida, USA, from 1,800 tonnes (1,984 US tons) of sand.

WOW

LARGEST SURFBOARD

Epic Big Board Ride and Visit Huntington Beach (both USA) worked together to set two records in honour of International Surfing Day on 20 Jun 2015. Made by a collaboration of surfboard- and boat-building experts, the Big Board is 12.83 m (42 ft 1.5 in) long. It was big enough to carry 66 surfers when it was tested off California, USA (left) – that's the **most people riding a surfboard**.

LARGEST PARASOL

Jiangxi Kuntak Industrial Co Limited (CHN) created a colourful umbrella that was 22.9 m (75 ft 1.5 in) in diameter – casting enough shade to cover one-and-a-half tennis courts! The 14.39-m-tall (47-ft 2.5-in) parasol was unfolded and measured in Jiangxi, China, on 3 Aug 2015.

LARGEST BEACH BALL

Polish supermarket chain Real bounced into the record books on 8 May 2012 with an inflatable ball that stretched 15.82 m (51 ft 10 in) across.

LARGEST BEACH TOWEL

In 2010, a towel covering 2,195.9 m² (23,636 sq ft) – an area big enough for 16 simultaneous games of beach volleyball – was rolled out in Gran Canaria, Spain. It was formed from more than 1,000 beach towels joined by Fateka SL on behalf of Compañía Cervecera de Canarias (ESP).

LARGEST HAMMOCK

To launch the gaming app *Paradise Bay*, King Digital Entertainment (UK) created a 20.8-m-long (68-ft 4-in) hammock with 196.3 m² (2,113 sq ft) of lounging space. Certificate in hand, GWR adjudicator Nicole Pando went to check out the humongous hammock at Liberty State Park in New Jersey, USA, on 2 Sep 2015.

AT THE CIRCUS

The original home of death-defying stunts, artistic displays and feats of strength, the big top is the place to go for record-breaking entertainment.

Amaluna

Luzia

20
Number of Cirque du Soleil shows around the world, eight of which were on tour as of Sep 2016.

Kurios

LARGEST CIRCUS ORGANIZATION

With close to 4,000 employees – including 1,300 full-time artists – Canada's Cirque du Soleil is the biggest circus organization. Since 1984, it has entertained more than 160 million people in some 60 countries.

Premiering in 2016, its latest show, *Luzia* (middle picture), is inspired by Mexico and the journey of the monarch butterfly (right), which has the **longest insect migration**.

THE HUMAN BULLET

One of the most explosive acts you'll see at the circus is the human cannonball. With at least 5,000 cannon shots under his belt, David Smith Jr (USA, left) – aka "The Bullet" – knows all about making an entrance... He not only holds the record for **farthest distance as a human cannonball** – 59.05 m (193 ft 8.8 in), but also the **greatest height**, soaring to 26 m (85 ft 3.6 in) in 2013.

LARGEST PERMANENT CIRCUS STRUCTURE (BY AREA)

As well as a record-breaking water park (see p.186), the Guangzhou Chimelong resort in China is also home to a record-breaking circus. The Chimelong International Circus covers an area of 11,435 m² (123,085 sq ft), including a 960-m² (10,333-sq-ft) show stage (above) and an auditorium that seats 7,100 spectators.

LONGEST-RUNNING CIRCUS

The first "Greatest Show on Earth" was put on by Barnum & Bailey in 1870. The circus merged with Ringling Bros Shows (right) in 1919 – a partnership that stands to this day. As of 2016, the circus had been entertaining the masses for 146 years.

FARTHEST TIGHTROPE WALK IN HIGH HEELS

On the set of TV show *Lo Show dei Record*, Russian circus artist Oxana Seroshtan walked along a wire for 15 m (49 ft 2.5 in) on 10 Jul 2014. If that weren't difficult enough, she performed the feat wearing high-heeled shoes! As per the rules, she was permitted to use a fan as a balancing aid. Her attempt doubled the distance of the former record.

LONGEST CAREER AS A RINGMASTER

Norman Barrett (UK) had been master of ceremonies at various circuses for 58 years as of Sep 2016. Originally from a farming background, Norman began by training the horses, before getting his big break as a ringmaster in 1957.

THEME PARKS

Thrills and spills are guaranteed as we take an adrenaline-fuelled tour of some record-breaking amusement parks and rides. Get ready to scream!

MOST THEME PARKS BASED ON A VIDEOGAME

As of 22 Feb 2016, there were 11 official fun parks based on the gaming app *Angry Birds*. Two are located in the UK, while China, Malaysia, Russia and Spain each have one. The rest can be found in Finland, which is the home of *Angry Birds'* creator, Rovio.

MOST RIDES IN AN AMUSEMENT PARK

Cedar Point in Sandusky, Ohio, USA, had 72 different mechanical rides as of 2014. As well as carousels, Ferris wheels and swing rides, the park is home to 17 roller-coasters, including the Wicked Twister, which is both the world's **fastest** (72 mph; 115.8 km/h) and **tallest** (215 ft; 65.5 m) **inverted roller-coaster**.

MOST VISITED THEME PARKS

Which amusement parks attracted the biggest crowds in 2015?

1. MAGIC KINGDOM

20,492,000
Florida, USA

2. DISNEYLAND

18,278,000
California, USA

In 2015, Disneyland Paris – better known as EuroDisney – was the ninth most visited theme park in the world. In Apr 2017, the resort will celebrate its 25th anniversary.

FIRST TOILET THEME PARK

South Korea's Restroom Cultural Park surrounds the toilet-shaped former home (above) of Sim Jae-duk, who founded the World Toilet Association. Demand is high, with up to 10,000 visitors per month! You can bet there's always a long line when you want to go...

HIGHEST THRILL RIDE

If you're afraid of heights, this one isn't for you... Located on the roof of the Canton Tower in Guangzhou, Guangdong, China, the Sky Drop elevates thrill-seekers 31 m (101 ft 8 in) up a mast. After briefly enjoying the view at 485 m (1,591 ft 2.4 in), riders plunge back to the roof. Gulp!

91 miles
The combined length of hot dogs eaten at Cedar Point each year. The dogs are washed down with 792,000 US gal (3 million litres) of soft drinks.

Source: AECOM/TEA, 2015 theme index

3. TOKYO DISNEYLAND
16,600,000
Tokyo, Japan

4. UNIVERSAL STUDIOS JAPAN
13,900,000
Osaka, Japan

5. TOKYO DISNEYSEA
13,600,000
Tokyo, Japan

WATER PARKS

Roller-coasters, big wheels and bumper cars are fun enough for landlubbers, but add a splash of H_2O into the mix and you get a whole new level of cool. As far as these record-setting attractions are concerned, the wetter the better!

926 ft
Length of the MASSIV water coaster that opened in 2016 (see opposite). That equates to two-and-a-half football fields!

TALLEST FLOWRIDING WAVE

It might look as if this guy is surfing, but he is, in fact, flowriding. The modern water sport combines a number of disciplines, including techniques from skateboarding, snowboarding and wakeboarding. On 24 Sep 2015, a machine known as "Da Wave" (left) produced what in the flowriding world is called a "sheet wave" that reached 3.5 m (11 ft 5.7 in) tall, at Splashworld in Monteux, France.

CONFIDENTIAL

RUMOUR HAS IT...

In 2017, the Universal Orlando Resort in Florida, USA, is expected to open a water park called Volcano Bay, set around a huge man-made volcano that gushes water (above).

MOST VISITED WATER PARK (CURRENT)

Based on the latest Global Attractions Attendance Report, compiled by the Themed Entertainment Association, Chimelong Water Park in Guangzhou, China, had an estimated 2,352,000 visitors in 2015. The attraction complex also boasts a safari area and bird park.

LARGEST WAVE POOL

Who said you can't surf in the city? The wave pool at Siam Park City in Bangkok, Thailand, covers an area of 13,600 m² (146,388 sq ft), according to the World Waterpark Association – about the same as 11 Olympic swimming pools! The pool can produce breakers up to 1.5 m (5 ft) tall.

TALLEST WATER COASTER

As verified on 16 Jun 2016, the new addition to Schlitterbahn Galveston Island Waterpark in Texas, USA, is MASSIV by name and massive by nature. At its highest point, the ride stands 24.86 m (81 ft 6.7 in) off the ground. Water coasters are distinguished from water slides by the riders' use of tubes or rafts, as well as other roller-coaster-inspired features, such as uphill "blaster" sections, spirals and water screens.

MOST SLIDES IN A WATER PARK (CURRENT)

Only opened on 1 Jul 2015, the Yinji Kaifeng Waterpark in Zhengzhou, Henan, China, has more twists and turns than your average water park. That's because it's home to 59 slides – some of which, such as its Racer Slides, include multiple lanes. By Sep 2016, the park intended for 47 of its rides to be outdoor and the remainder to be indoor.

TOP 10: FASTEST ROLLER-COASTERS

Little can match the adrenaline rush you get from the slow climbs, rapid plunges and head-over-heels loops on a roller-coaster... And in the case of these speedy rides, it will all be over before you know it!

FORMULA ROSSA

1

149.1 mph (240 km/h)

You'd anticipate a faster-than-average roller-coaster when it's designed by Ferrari – and the Formula Rossa at Ferrari World in Abu Dhabi, UAE, doesn't disappoint! The carriages are built to resemble F1 cars and, with an acceleration of 0–100 km/h (0–62 mph) in two seconds, they feel like racing cars too. The world's **fastest roller-coaster** uses a hydraulic launcher to catapult its cars on to a 2.2-km (1.4-mi) track inspired by the Autodromo Nazionale Monza circuit in Italy.

KINGDA KA

128 mph (206 km/h)

Located in Jackson, New Jersey, the USA's fastest coaster hits its peak speed in 3.5 sec. It's also the **tallest roller-coaster**, at 456 ft (138.9 m).

2

TOP THRILL DRAGSTER

120 mph (193.1 km/h)

When opened in 2003, this Ohio, USA, ride was both the fastest and the tallest roller-coaster, at 420 ft (128 m) high. Themed around Top Fuel drag racers, it is all over in just 17 sec.

3

DODONPA

106.9 mph (172 km/h)

This Japanese coaster offers a face-wobbling dose of g-force. Going 0–172 km/h (0–106.9 mph) in 1.8 sec, Dodonpa has been the **fastest-accelerating roller-coaster** since 2001.

4

KEEP ON ROLLING, ROLLING...

Forget speed – the world's longest roller-coasters are all about going the distance...

1. STEEL DRAGON 2000
8,133 ft 2.4 in (2,478.9 m)
Nagashima Spa Land (JPN)

2. ULTIMATE
7,442 ft (2,268.3 m)
Lightwater Valley (UK)

SUPERMAN: ESCAPE FROM KRYPTON
100 mph (160.9 km/h)

Is it a bird? Is it a plane? No, it's the joint fifth-fastest roller-coaster. This 28-sec flight through the Man of Steel's Fortress of Solitude is just one of 19 coasters to be enjoyed at the Magic Mountain resort in Valencia, California, USA – that's the **most roller-coasters in one theme park**.

=5

TOWER OF TERROR II
100 mph (160.9 km/h)

Opened in 1997, the original Tower of Terror at Dreamworld park in Queensland, Australia, was the world's **first coaster to hit 100 mph**. Its successor (pictured), launched in 2010, is even more terrifying. Now riders face downwards and experience weightlessness for 6.5 sec of the ride.

=5

FURY 325
95 mph (152.9 km/h)

Opened in North Carolina, USA, in 2015, the newest addition to this top 10 is a "giga coaster" – that's a coaster with a drop of 300–400 ft (91–122 m) as part of a full circuit. The theme of the ride is said to be a hornet chasing its prey.

=7

STEEL DRAGON 2000
95 mph (152.9 km/h)

Japan's Steel Dragon is joint-seventh in the speed stakes, but it does hold the No.1 spot for track length (see bar below). Its name is derived from the Chinese calendar, as when this ride opened in 2000, it was the Year of the Dragon. To withstand frequent earthquakes, its steel content is much higher than most other coasters.

=7

MILLENNIUM FORCE
93 mph (149.7 km/h)

When opened in 2000 at Cedar Point in Sandusky, Ohio, USA – also home to the Top Thrill Dragster (No.3) – this was the world's fastest coaster. Although it has since lost that title, it still holds the honour of being the **first giga coaster**.

9

LEVIATHAN
92 mph (148.1 km/h)

The twists and turns of this ride, inspired by its sea monster namesake, last for 3 min 28 sec. Towering over Canada's Wonderland in Ontario, it is the country's tallest and fastest coaster.

10

Source: rcdb.com, correct as of May 2016; only includes rides currently in operation

3. BEAST
7,359 ft (2,243 m)
Kings Island (USA)

4. FUJIYAMA
6,708 ft 8.4 in (2,044.8 m)
Fuji-Q Highland (JPN)

5. FURY 325
6,602 ft (2,012.2 m)
Carowinds (USA)

Top that!
The world's largest takeaway pizza is so huge that the delivery vans have a special compartment mounted on the roof to transport it.

CONSUME

PERSONAL TECH

From smartphones and tablets to smartwatches and MP3s, it can be hard to imagine life in the 21st century without these record-setting gadgets.

BEST-SELLING SMARTPHONE BRAND (RETAIL, CURRENT)

Samsung (KOR) sold approximately 266,730,800 handsets in 2015. Its latest model, the Galaxy S7 (above), is designed to withstand splashes and is even capable of total immersion, as demonstrated at its launch (main picture), for up to 30 min. Samsung's closest smartphone rivals are shown in the table below.

55 hr
Music playback time afforded by the Galaxy S7's battery. That equates to 28 hr of talk time, 14 hr of wi-fi use or 16 hr of video playback.

TOP 5 SMARTPHONE BRANDS

BRAND	UNITS SOLD
Samsung (KOR)	266,730,800
iPhone (USA, above)	201,151,700
Huawei (CHN, right)	87,331,400
Xiaomi (CHN)	68,918,500
LG (KOR)	51,777,200

Source: Euromonitor International, 2015 retail sales data; figures retrieved on 22 Aug 2016

Samsung isn't all about consumer technology; the company also constructed the 828-m-high (2,716-ft 6-in) Burj Khalifa in Dubai, UAE – the world's **tallest building**.

BEST-SELLING BRAND OF...

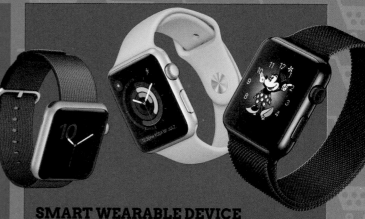

TABLET
iPad: 44,539,600 units sold

SMART WEARABLE DEVICE
Apple Watch: 8,719,700 units sold

PORTABLE PLAYER
iPod: 21,906,800 units sold

eREADER
Kindle: 9,503,400 units sold

Source: All sales records based on Euromonitor International retail sales data for 2015; figures retrieved on 22 Aug 2016

MOST VALUABLE BRAND
According to Interbrand's annual "Best Brands" ranking, in 2016 tech giant Apple (USA) increased its value by 43% on the previous year. They calculated the iPhone and Mac maker to be worth an extraordinary $170.2 bn (£112.1 bn). This put Apple far ahead of second-place Google, valued at $120.3 bn (£79.2 bn).

THE END OF TANGLED EARPHONES?
One of the coolest new gadgets to appear at 2016's CES tech show in Las Vegas, Nevada, USA, were Bragi's cable-free earbuds, called the Dash. They have been a while coming, having raised more than $3.3 m (£2 m) on Kickstarter in 2014. As well as removing the hassle of detangling wires, this innovative audio device lets you store up to 1,000 songs that can be played independent of any connection and offers real-time feedback, such as your heart rate, during exercise.

FAST FOOD

Stomach rumbling? Fast food has been helping to fight hunger pangs since the 1920s. Today, these chain restaurants are some of the world's most familiar brands, but the fantastic food here is anything but familiar...

50
Years since McDonald's introduced its most iconic burger, the Big Mac. Two new versions were trialled in 2016: the "Grand Mac" and the "Mac Jr".

LARGEST PIZZA ON SALE
If you and 100 friends ever have a hankering for some "za", call Big Mama's & Papa's Pizzeria in Los Angeles, California, USA. The "Giant Sicilian" on their menu is 20.25 sq ft (1.88 m²) – that's the same as nearly 19 open copies of this book! The only catch is that they need 24 hours to prepare it.

BEYOND THE BURGER
WE RUSTLE UP A FEW MORE FAST-FOOD FEATS FROM AROUND THE GLOBE

LARGEST SERVING OF FRIED CHICKEN
On 23 Sep 2011 in Nakatsu, Japan, radio station NOAS FM produced the ultimate mega-bucket of crispy chicken for the fourth Karaage Festival. It tipped the scales at 1,076 kg (2,372 lb 2.72 oz).

The first McDonald's "drive-thru" was set up in Sierra Vista, Arizona, USA, in 1975. It served soldiers from a local military base, who weren't allowed to leave their vehicles while in uniform.

MOST EXPENSIVE HOT DOG

Now this is what you call an *haute dog*... The "Juuni Ban", sold by Tokyo Dog in Seattle, Washington, USA, contains everything from caviar and black truffle to Wagyu beef. It had a price tag of $169 (£101) as of 2014.

LARGEST COLLECTION OF RESTAURANT TOYS

Fast-food joints aren't all about the chow... Nobody has amassed more of the giveaway toys than Percival R Lugue (PHL), who owned 10,000 when last counted on 4 Nov 2014. His collectables hail from a wide range of diners, including Wendy's, Burger King, Jollibee and McDonald's.

MOST BIG MACS EATEN

For most of us, a McDonald's meal is a convenient snack or maybe a birthday treat. For Donald Gorske (USA), however, they are a way of life. Forty-four years after he started his mission to eat a Big Mac every day, he bit into no. 28,788 on 24 Aug 2016. "As long as they keep making them, I'm going to keep eating them," Donald said. There's no doubt that he's lovin' it!

LARGEST BURRITO

CANIRAC La Paz (MEX) wrapped fish with onion, chilli and refried beans into a single flour tortilla to create a 5,799.44-kg (12,785-lb 9.2-oz) burrito in 2010.

LARGEST ONION BHAJI

In 2011, students from Bradford College and Prashad restaurant (both UK) made a behemoth bhaji weighing 102.2 kg (225 lb 4.9 oz).

SOMETHING SWEET

Savoury fans might want to turn the page because this feature is dedicated to sugar-coated records. For those with a sweet tooth, meanwhile, be prepared to drool...

LARGEST COLLECTION OF CANDY WRAPPERS

While most of us are only interested in the candy, Milan Lukich Valdivia (PER) earned a record by collecting the colourful packaging. By 23 Dec 2015, he had 5,065 wrappers from 49 different countries.

LARGEST PEZ DISPENSER SCULPTURE

The Aberdeen Centre in Richmond, British Columbia, Canada, built a 1.54-m-tall (5-ft) replica of the Elizabeth Tower on 30 Jun 2016. The UK landmark is often referred to as "Big Ben"; however, this is actually the name of the bell *inside* the tower. The model was made out of emoji-faced PEZ dispensers (see inset right).

SUGAR RUSH
THE FASTEST CANDY SORTERS WITH CHOPSTICKS

30 M&M'S/SMARTIES
Yinger Guan (CHN)
31.50 sec

30 JELLY BEANS
Silvio Sabba (ITA)
23.39 sec

30 JELLY BABIES
Stephen Kish (UK)
27.42 sec

According to Wrigley, more than 200 million Skittles candies are made every day. That's more than the populations of France, Italy and the UK combined!

100 YEARS OF KISSES

LARGEST SKITTLES MOSAIC

The Australian Dry July Foundation assembled this colourful confection in Sydney, New South Wales, Australia, on 24 Jul 2014. Covering an area of 6.78 m² (73 sq ft), the work comprised more than 50,000 Skittles sweets. It was inspired by Leonardo da Vinci's iconic portrait, the *Mona Lisa* – the original of which is housed at the Louvre gallery in Paris, France.

LARGEST INDIVIDUAL CHOCOLATE

Put this Hershey's Kiss on a pair of scales and you'd need about three African elephants on the other side to balance it out! Weighing in at 30,540 lb (13,852.7 kg), the killer Kiss was made to celebrate the confectioner's 100th anniversary in 2007.

MOST MENTOS/SODA FOUNTAINS

This is when science gets fun... and messy! Dropping Mentos into a fizzy drink radically speeds up the release of CO_2 bubbles from the liquid, resulting in a sweet geyser. Chupa Chups Industrial Mexicana and Perfetti Van Melle (both MEX) set off 4,334 fountains at once on 15 Nov 2014.

HOW PEZ GOT A-HEAD

PEZ is probably most famous for its dispensers. Since it introduced its character heads in 1955 to attract a younger audience, the candy-holders have included everyone from the Muppets and Bilbo Baggins to Buzz Lightyear (far right). PEZ says its best-selling dispenser is Santa Claus (near right), of which there have been many variants.

FIZZY FEATS

Earning Guinness World Records titles can be thirsty work – but that's certainly not an issue for these beverage-based records.

TOP 5 SOFT DRINK BRANDS

Coca-Cola (USA)	$45.69 bn (£31.77 bn)
Pepsi (USA, right)	$16.18 bn (£11.24 bn)
Sprite (USA)	$9.58 bn (£6.46 bn)
Red Bull (AUT)	$9.04 bn (£6.09 bn)
Gatorade (USA, left)	$8.28 bn (£5.58 bn)

Source: Euromonitor International, 2015 off-trade sales data; figures retrieved on 20 Apr 2016

MOST CANS STUCK TO THE HEAD WITH AIR SUCTION

"Can Head", aka Jamie Keeton (USA), held eight soda cans on his head solely using air suction on Chinese TV show *CCTV – Guinness World Records Special* on 11 Jan 2016. He first noticed his skin's unusual quality as a child when toys would randomly stick to him. As far as his doctor is concerned, Jamie is the only person in the USA with the mystery condition. Can Head now makes his living touring the world to demonstrate his amazing talent.

LARGEST ALUMINIUM CAN SCULPTURE

The Junior Chamber International Toyohashi recreated Yoshida Castle in the shadow of the real fortification in Toyohashi Park, Aichi, Japan, on 21 Sep 2013. The final structure used a total of 104,840 drinks cans that had been collected from the residents of Toyohashi City. Excluding its base, the highest point of the fizzy fortress was 5 m (16 ft 4 in).

Using just his beak, Zac the macaw opened 35 soda cans in one minute in 2012. It's not his only party trick – see another of his records on p.29.

HIGHEST CLIFF JUMP

As well as being 2015's **best-selling energy drinks brand (off-trade volume)** according to Euromonitor International data as of 26 May 2016, Red Bull is also synonymous with action sports. In 2015, cliff jumper Laso Schaller (CHE, b. BRA, above) leapt 58.5 m (191 ft 11 in) into a natural pool in Maggia, Switzerland.

MOST DRINKS CANS BROKEN WITH A WHIP IN THREE MINUTES

It might not be the most practical way of getting into your soda, but it sure looks cool! Sharp-eyed Adam Winrich (USA) – who has whipped up a number of records over the years (see below) – destroyed 23 drinks cans on the set of *Lo Show dei Record* in Milan, Italy, in 2009.

267

Whip cracks performed by Adam Winrich (above) in 60 sec on 7 May 2016 – the most bullwhip cracks in one minute.

MOST CANS BALANCED ON THE HEAD

On 5 Jun 2007, headstrong John Evans (UK) supported 429 cans of 7 Up on a board, with a combined weight of 173 kg (381 lb 6 oz), in Ilkeston, Derbyshire, UK. It's not his only drink-based balancing act (see a few others below)...

EVANS ALMIGHTY!

More records for which John Evans kept a level head...

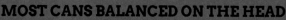

BEER KEGS	MILK CRATES	PINT GLASSES
11	96	235

📷 THE BIG PICTURE

Davide Andreani (ITA) is one canny collector... As of 14 Aug 2013, he owned 10,558 Coca-Cola cans from 87 different countries, making his the **largest collection of same-brand soft drink cans**. Davide obtained the first in 1979, when he was just five years old. He actually owns many more duplicates that don't count towards the total. He uses these for trading to fill in gaps in his collection.

"The most valuable cans are those produced for a special moment, like gold cans for anniversaries. But these cans are very limited and very rare." *Davide Andreani*

COOL KICKS

Trainers, sneakers, treads, kicks... Whatever you call your sports shoes, it's time to celebrate a few fantastic footwear feats!

4 years 85 days
Length of time Joshua Mueller (below) can go if he wears a different pair of Converse shoes each day!

COOL KICK COLLECTIONS

Joshua Mueller (USA, above) owned the **largest collection of Converse shoes** – 1,546 sets at the last official count in 2012. Fellow shoe fan Jordy Geller (USA, right), meanwhile, boasts the **largest collection of sneakers** overall: 2,388 pairs as of 2012.

TOP 5 KIDS' SHOE BRANDS OF 2015

NIKE (USA)
$3,749,340,700
(£2.57 bn)

ADIDAS (DEU)
$1,637,467,300
(£1.10 bn)

PAYLESS SHOESOURCE (USA)
$853,399,500
(£575.6 m)

Converse All Stars really took off with the endorsement of basketball player Charles "Chuck" Taylor (left) in 1921. In his honour, the shoes now bear his name.

BEST-SELLING KIDS' SHOE BRAND

Nike (USA) sold an estimated $3,749,340,700 (£2.57 bn) worth of children's shoes in 2015, according to Euromonitor International figures retrieved on 27 Apr 2016 (see top 5 brands, below). Adults couldn't get enough of the "swoosh" either, buying $27,395,441,700 (£18.83 bn) worth of Nike shoes in 2015, making it the current **largest footwear brand** overall.

I THINK I'VE GOT A STONE IN MY SHOE...

If you thought that your last pair of sneakers were pricey, think again! A pair of one-off shoes, called the "Fire Monkey", were customized with 18-karat gold and studded with diamonds and sapphires. Manufactured by luxury brand Bicion and sneaker designer Dan Gamache (both USA), the final price tag was $4 m (£2.4 m) when they went on sale in 2016 on behalf of charity Soles4Souls. By Sep 2016, the blingy treads had yet to sell.

LARGEST SHOE

A scaled-up Superga 2750 (below) measured 6.40 m (20 ft 11.9 in) long and 1.65 m (5 ft 4.9 in) high. It was made by fashion firm Electric sekki (HKG) as part of Superga's Chinese launch in 2013. The **largest hiking boot**, on the other *foot*, is a 7.14-m-long (23-ft 5-in), 4.2-m-tall (13-ft 9-in) leather boot (right), made by Schuh Marke (DEU) in 2006.

SKECHERS (USA)
$530,622,700
(£357.9 m)

TIMBERLAND (USA)
$502,407,800
(£338.8 m)

Source: Euromonitor International, 2015 retail sales data; figures retrieved on 27 Apr 2016

KIDS' CHOICE AWARDS

The Nickelodeon Kids' Choice Awards (KCAs) have been celebrating the best of pop culture, as voted for by kids, since 1986. Originally part of the *Big Ballot* TV show, the now-independent annual awards ceremony attracts the most popular stars from movies, music, the internet and beyond to vie for coveted orange blimps. It is one of the most eagerly anticipated – or for slime-hating celebrities, dreaded – events of the year.

MOST KCAs WON BY A MALE SINGER

Justin Bieber (CAN) has won a total of five "blimps". His latest is for Favorite Male Singer in 2016 off the back of his fourth album *Purpose* (2015), which includes hits such as "What Do You Mean?" and "Sorry". He's also had the "honour" of being slimed (see "Slime on!") at the 2012 Kids' Choice Awards ceremony.

Slime on!

Whether it's the host, the winners or guests – or even the entire audience in 1992 – nobody is safe from the infamous green goo. In 2016, online stars Cameron Dallas and Taylor Caniff (right) and girl group Fifth Harmony were among the victims.

MOST KCAs WON BY A FEMALE

Singer/actor Selena Gomez (USA) has won nine KCAs to date. Five were earned for her starring role in Disney's *Wizards of Waverly Place*. She also holds the record for **most KCAs won by a female singer**: three.

Nickelodeon's trademark green goo certainly gets around... On 26 Sep 2014, Nickelodeon Australia slimed 3,309 people at Slimefest – the **most people gunged in 24 hours**.

AS OF 2016, TWO MOVIE FRANCHISES ARE TIED ON THREE KCAs: HOW DO THEY COMPARE?

THE HUNGER GAMES

Years won: 2013–15

Total theatrical releases: 4

Success rate: 75%

Lead character: Katniss Everdeen

Origin: Books; first published in 2008

ALVIN AND THE CHIPMUNKS

Years won: 2008, 2010, 2012

Total theatrical releases: 5

Success rate: 60%

Lead characters: Alvin, Simon, Theodore

Origin: TV cartoon; first shown in 1961

MOST KCAs WON BY A GAME SERIES

No other videogame has been more successful with KCA voters than *Just Dance*, with five wins in the Favorite Video Game category, in 2011–14 and 2016. The latest victory was for *Just Dance 2016* – the seventh title in the main line of the **best-selling dance videogame series**.

MOST KCAs WON BY AN INDIVIDUAL

Will Smith (USA) may have got his big break as the "Fresh Prince", but today he is the "king" of the KCAs. Across nearly two decades, he won an unmatched 10 "blimps" for his singing and acting. His most recent was Favorite Movie Actor in 2009 for *Hancock* (2008).

TOP 10: ENTERTAINMENT BRANDS

Every year, US market researcher Smarty Pants asks families what's hot and what's not. Topics vary from candy and fashion to tech and websites, all of which are then given a "Kidfinity" score (see top right). Here we focus on your favourite franchises from the world of entertainment.

MINIONS   1
Kidfinity score: 832

The mischievous Minions were 2015's leading entertainers, ranking 14th in the full Kidfinity list. The year saw the release of their first self-titled film, which achieved the **highest-grossing opening weekend for an animated movie (global)**. Fans will be delighted to hear that *Despicable Me 3* and *Minions 2* are both underway for 2017 and 2018, respectively. Minions, *tulaliloo ti amo*!

LEGO®   2
Kidfinity score: 811

LEGO might be the world's **largest construction toy brand,** but the plastic bricks have moved far beyond the toy box, with a growing legacy of films, games and books. Their infinite potential to tie in to other mega-franchises (e.g. No.4) means that LEGO always stays bang up to date.

MARIO   3
Kidfinity score: 783

Videogame stars don't come much more iconic than this Nintendo giant. Mario made his debut in the 1981 arcader *Donkey Kong*. In 2015, fans got to create their very own levels in the Mushroom Kingdom for the very first time, in the Wii U title *Super Mario Maker*.

LEGO MINECRAFT   4
Kidfinity score: 759

This killer collaboration, combining virtual blocks with real ones, was a dead cert for success. The line's largest set to date is The Fortress (below), launched in 2016; it has 984 pieces.

WHAT KIDS WANT...   Which brands topped the overall list in 2015?

OREO
Kidfinity score: 880

M&M'S
Kidfinity score: 863

Smarty Pants works out its "Kidfinity" scores based on awareness and popularity, using a scale of 0 to 1,000. In 2015's poll, 7,054 children and their parents took part.

MINECRAFT
5

Kidfinity score: 740

Mojang's mining mega-hit struck gold on its release in 2009 – and gamers have been "digging" the **best-selling indie game** ever since. This open-world title became more real-world in 2016 with the arrival of two virtual-reality editions: one for the Gear VR and another for the Oculus Rift.

SPONGEBOB SQUAREPANTS
6

Kidfinity score: 727

Who lives in a pineapple under the sea? SpongeBob SquarePants, of course! The cheery Nickelodeon star appeared in the ninth season of his hit cartoon in 2016, which first aired in 1999.

ANGRY BIRDS
7

Kidfinity score: 712

Back in 2012, *Angry Birds* became the **first gaming series to reach 1 billion downloads**. Its popularity resurged with the release of its own movie in 2016, which became the **highest-grossing animated film based on a videogame** (see p.38).

MARVEL AVENGERS
8

Kidfinity score: 697

Comic books, movies (including the **highest-grossing superhero movie**), videogames, TV series, toys, apps... Is there any form of media that Hulk and co *can't* smash? The next instalment in the main film series is *Avengers: Infinity War*, slated for a 2018 release.

LOONEY TUNES
9

Kidfinity score: 695

Proving that the classics still know how to entertain us, Looney Tunes has been on our screens for more than 85 years. There's a good chance that Bugs Bunny (right), Tweety and Wile E Coyote will be raising a smile for many more years to come – so that's *not* all, folks!

LEGO FRIENDS
10

Kidfinity score: 684

The residents of Heartlake City have been keeping LEGO fans amused since 2012. As well as intricate sets, such as the Adventure Camp Tree House (below), the range has spawned a long-running series of webisodes.

Source: Smarty Pants, 2015; *Kidscreen*

NETFLIX

Kidfinity score: 857

iPAD
Kidfinity score: 856

HERSHEY'S
Kidfinity score: 856

BLOCKBUSTER CHALLENGES

Now that you've read about the records achieved by celebrities and other people, how about trying to set one of your own? The four record titles here have been inspired by features in *Blockbusters! 2017*. They are all making their first appearance in this book, so you can be one of the first to attempt them. Good luck!

MOST UNDERWEAR PUT ON IN ONE MINUTE
(TEAM OF TWO)

Along with capes, belts and boots, underpants on the outside are a classic part of many a superhero outfit. Now you too can strike your best Superman pose for this *briefs* encounter! The catch is that you have to work as a team, with one person stepping into the underwear and the other pulling them on. Sound easy? You'll be surprised at how much coordination this involves!

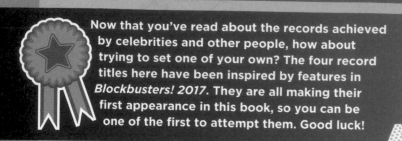

FASTEST TIME TO MATCH 20 EMOJI PAIRS

We now use emoji to communicate more than ever, but this record isn't about keeping in touch – it's a test of memory! Just as with the traditional game that uses standard playing cards, you must turn over two cards at a time until you have found all the pairs. But rather than matching numbers, in this case you're searching for identical emoji. There's both a physical and a digital version of the game available on our website (see below).

CHECK OUT THE RULES!

Before taking on any of these blockbuster challenges, make sure you head to **www.guinnessworldrecords.com/blockbusters** for full guidelines and useful tips. You'll also find lots of extra *Blockbusters!* goodness on the website, including activities, quizzes and amazing photos!

Comic-book stars such as Superman wear their underpants on the outside because early superheroes were inspired by the attire of circus acts such as strongmen.

MOST SOFT TOYS CAUGHT BLINDFOLDED IN ONE MINUTE
(TEAM OF TWO)

The second of the team challenges requires one thrower and one catcher; just be aware that the latter will be blindfolded! The aim of the game is to catch – and just as importantly *hold on to* – as many plush toys as possible in a minute. For the thrower, the secrets to success for this record are an accurate aim and good communication, while for the catcher, it's all about listening skills and reaction times. Before you begin, you and your team-mate may also want to think strategically about which toys you use...

FASTEST TIME TO STACK 20 LEGO® BRICKS IN A RIGHT-ANGLE TOWER

Building a tower of 20 LEGO bricks might sound simple, but don't be fooled... When you're up against the clock, every fumbled brick or slip of concentration can eat up valuable milliseconds. Plus, a word of warning: this staggered stack can get very unstable towards the top! There are two versions of this record – one using normal-sized bricks (right) and another using large LEGO bricks (left). Check out the rules for both on the *Blockbusters!* website (see opposite) before you start building.

INDEX

Bold entries in the index indicate a main entry on a topic. **BOLD CAPITALS** indicate an entire chapter.

A

Action Comics 31
action figures 166–167
Action Man 16, 166
actors & actresses:
    cameo appearances 24, 47; connected 68; earnings 113; Facebook likes 87; profitable 11; Twitter followers 91; Wikipedia views 76
Adele 78, 79, 94, 95
Adidas 202
advertising space 75
albums: sales 79, 95; streaming 81
Alibaba Group 74
Alice in Wonderland **102–103**
Alice Through the Looking Glass (movie) 103
alien-invasion movies 34–35
The Aliens Are Coming! 34–35
Allegiant (movie) 112
Allen, Sean 159
Alvin and the Chipmunks (cartoon) 56, 205
The Amazing Spider-Man (movie) 59
The Amazing World of Gumball (cartoon) 57
Amazon 74, 109
American football 179
"Anaconda" (song) 78
Andersen, Hans Christian 111
Andreani, Davide 200–201
Angry Birds (game) 38, 184, 207
Angry Birds (movie) 38
animals: land mine detectors 44; LEGO sculptures 129; music written for 44; tricks 28, 29; Wall Street investors 45; zoos and aquariums 176–177; *see also individual entries*
animated movies: awards 35, 50;

box-office 18, 19, 20, 29, 50, 57, 111, 206, 207; budgets 59; game-to-movie 38–39, 207; ratings 111; stereoscopic 3D 35; widest release 29
animated TV shows 46–47
Ant-Man (movie) 24
apes & monkeys 12, 106
Apple 193; Apple Music 81; Apple Watch 193
apps 16, 38, 39, 88, 93, 147, 160, 181
aquariums 176, 177
arcade machines 16, 174, 175
Armor Hero 167
Ascendant (movie) 112
Assassin's Creed (movie) 38
asteroids 42
Astro Sloth 69
astronauts 89, 161, 168
At the Beach 180–181
At the Circus 182–183
athletes: Facebook likes 86–87, 89; Twitter followers 89, 91; Wikipedia views 76
auctions: books and illustrations 104, 109; comics 25; eBay 74–75; figurines 16; hair clippings 74, 75; toy cars 148
augmented-reality (AR) technology 147
authors: best-selling 98, 99, 108; billion-dollar author 109; children's 98–101; earnings 98, 109, 112
Autodesk 68
Avatar (movie) 58
The Avengers (movie) 10, 24, 76
Avengers: Age of Ultron (movie) 11, 58, 59, 167, 213
Avengers: Infinity War (movie) 207
Avengers toys 167
awards: Emmy Awards 47; Grammy Awards 94; Kids' Choice Awards 56, 204–205; Laurence Olivier Awards 115; Oscars 35, 91, 95; Visual Effects Society Awards 50
Azaria, Hank 47

B

"Baby" (song) 95
Baby Cha-Cha 68
Bachelor, Andrew 93
Bacon, Kevin 68
"Bacon number" concept 68
"Bad Blood" (song) 78
Badger, Badger, Badger 68

"Bailando" (song) 95
ball machine, K'NEX 134
balloons, objects lifted by 18
Barnhart, Alicia 179
Barnum & Bailey 183
Barrett, Norman 183
baseball cards 75
Basford, Johanna 104
basketball 70, 71; parrots 29
Batman (movie) 30
Batman: Arkham (game series) 171
Batman Begins (movie) 30
Batman Forever (movie) 30
Batman v Superman 30–31
Batman v Superman: Dawn of Justice (movie) 30, 59
Batmobile 130, 132
Baxter, Michael 47
BB-8 63, 162, 166
beach balls 181
beach towels 181
The Beano (comic) 121
bears 107
Beast roller-coaster 189
Beatrice, Princess 74
Beauty and the Beast (movie) 110
Beauty Behind the Madness (album) 81
Beck, Hans 166
Beckett, Richard 162
Beckham, David 87, 89
Beckham, Victoria 57
Beer, Albert 163
beer kegs 199
Ben 10 **54–55**
Ben 10: Protector of Earth (game) 55
Benenson, Fred 83
Berg, Bryan 145
Bergensten, Jens 143
"Best Song Ever" (song) 79
Beyoncé 81, 88
The BFG (movie) 114, 115
Bicion 203
Bieber, Justin 75, 78, 80, 81, 87, 89, 90, 95, 204
The Big Bang Theory (TV series) 77
Big Friendly Giant 114, 115
Big Hero 6 (movie) 44, 50
Big Macs 194, 195
The Big Picture: DanTDM 64–65
The Big Picture: Largest Coca-Cola Can Collection 200–201
The Big Picture: Largest Loop-the-Loop 150–151
The Big Picture: Largest NERF Gun 164–165
The Big Picture: Largest Rubik's Cube 136–137
The Big Picture: Largest Superman Collection 32–33

The Big Picture: Largest Winnie the Pooh Collection 118–119
bikes, dogs on 28
The Billion-View Club (YouTube videos) 94–95
Black Death 117
black holes 42
Blake, Sir Quentin 99, 104, 114
Blanchett, Cate 106
"Blank Space" (song) 78, 94, 95
Blazing Star (game) 68
blindfolded: basketball shots 70; soft toys, catching 209
Blixt, Claes 145
Blockbuster Challenges 208–209
Bloodhound SSC 135
Blum, Steve 54, 153
books 98–119; adult colouring books 104; dystopian fiction 112–113; fairy tales 110–111; kids' book villains 124–125; valuable 102, 109; vloggers 98; *see also authors; comics; and individual titles*
Books Round-Up 98–99
bookstores, online 74
BotCon 171
Bowie, David 57, 78
Breakout (game) 175
Bricktopia 128–129
Brolsma, Gary 69
Broomhall, Ashley 15
BROWSE 60–95
Bruce, Chloe 15
Bryant, Kobe 145
bullwhip cracks 199
Burj Khalifa 193
burritos 195
Burroughs, Edgar Rice 59, 106
Burrows, Simon and Irene 102
Burton, Tim 103
Bush, George W 77

C

cable TV, US 50, 51
Caine, Michael 47
cakes 102
Calaway, Mark 52
calendars 103
Camberis, Jason 175
Cameron, James 58
candies 196–197
Candy Crush Saga (game) 154
candy wrappers 196
Caniff, Taylor 204
Capaldi, Peter 49
Captain America & The Avengers 10–11

Captain America: Civil War (movie) 10, 24, 45
Captain America: The First Avenger (movie) 10
Captain America: The Winter Soldier (movie) 11
Captain Britain (comic) 122
card games 144–145; deck sizes 145; digital games 144; trading cards 16, 144, 145
Card Play 144–145
card towers 145
Carpenter, Doug 16
Carroll, Lewis 102–103

cars: K'NEX models 135; loop-the-loop 150–151; model cars 148–149; motorsport 179
cartoons: Kids' Choice Awards 56–57; *see also animated movies*
Cassell, Tom 66
Castañeda, Mariand Castrejón 63
The Cat in the Hat (book) 100
cats: Grumpy Cat 69; piano-playing 44; tricks 29
Cedar Point amusement park 184
Cena, John 53, 87
Chan, Jackie 87
Charlie and the Chocolate Factory (movie) 103, 115
chelonians 23
"Chewbacca Mom" 86
Chimelong International Circus 183
Chimelong Ocean Kingdom 176
Chimelong Water Park 186
chimpanzees 45
Chitty Chitty Bang Bang (movie) 115
Cho, Joy 93
chocolate 197
chopsticks, sorting candies with 196
circus 182–183
Cirque du Soleil 182
Clemmett, Sam 109
cliff jumping 199
Close, Glenn 47
clownfish 23
Coca-Cola 198; largest can collection 200–201

Collins, Suzanne 113
colouring books 104
Comic Books Round-Up 120–121
Comic-Con International 171, 173
comics 120–123; artists 121; characters 172–173; conventions 171, 172–173; manga 121, 171; publishers 120, 121; *Superman* 31; valuable 25, 31
Comiket 171
Connors, Lily 48
Console Gaming 152–153

conspiracy theories 35
CONSUME 190–207
Conventions 142, **170–171**, 172–173
Converse shoes 202, 203
Cool Constructions 134–135
Cool Kicks 202–203
Cornelius, Robert 84
cosplay 170, 171
Courtney, Lisa 146
Craig, Daniel 58
cranes 13
craters, lunar 43
Criscione, Jesse James 121
Crossy Road (game) 154, 155
crowd events: Batman 30; Ben 10 54; comic-book characters 172–173; dancing robots 162; deer antlers 93; Doctor Who 49; Dr Seuss 101; Etch A Sketch 138; ghosts 26; Harlem Shake 69; human symbols 82; ice bucket challenge 69; martial arts 13; Minecraft 143; PAC-Man 175; Peter Pan 111; pinball 174; selfies 85; smiley (emoji) 82; Star Trek 41; Superman 31; tea parties 103; toy pistol fight 138

INDEX

Worn by Iron Man, aka Tony Stark, the Hulkbuster armour that inspired this cosplay suit made its movie debut in 2015's *Avengers: Age of Ultron*.

INDEX

COUNTRY CODES

PICTURE CREDITS

Front: Pokémon, Sony Pictures; **Cover:** Cartoon Network, DreamWorks/Alamy, Disney/Pixar/Alamy, Warner Bros; **Back cover & spine:** Microsoft/Mojang, Sony, EmojiOne; **2/3:** Alamy, Lucasfilm, Disney/Pixar; **4/5:** Alamy, Alamy, EmojiOne, Alamy, Nickelodeon/Alamy; **6/7:** Paul Michael Hughes/GWR; **8/9:** Disney/Pixar, DreamWorks/Alamy, Alamy, Disney, Nickelodeon, Twentieth Century Fox/Rex; **10/11:** Alamy, Alamy, Alamy, Alamy, Alamy, Alamy; **12/13:** DreamWorks, Zuofu Xiang/BBC, Shutterstock, Shutterstock, Shutterstock, Alamy, Shutterstock, Alamy; **14/15:** Lucasfilm, Shutterstock, Rex, Lucasfilm; **16/17:** Vectis, Disney, Alamy, Alamy, Alamy, Lucasfilm, Lucasfilm; **18/19:** Disney/Pixar/Alamy, National Geographic, Disney/Pixar, Disney/Pixar, Pixar, Pixar/Alamy, Pixar, Shutterstock; **20/21:** Disney/Alamy, Disney/Pixar, Disney/Pixar, Disney/Alamy, Rex, Alamy; **22/23:** Shutterstock, Alamy, Alamy, Disney/Pixar, Disney/Pixar, Alamy, Alamy, Disney/Pixar, Disney/Pixar, Alamy, Disney/Pixar, Alamy; **24/25:** 20th Century Fox, 20th Century Fox/Alamy, 20th Century Fox/Alamy, 20th Century Fox/Alamy; **26/27:** Dave Mangels, Chris Polk, Sony Pictures; **28/29:** Kevin Scott Ramos/GWR, Universal Pictures/Alamy, Universal Pictures/Alamy, Carley Garantziotis/GWR, James Ellerker/GWR; **30/31:** Kevin Scott Ramos/GWR, Warner Bros/Alamy, Alamy, Alamy, Alamy, Warner Bros/Alamy, Alamy; **32/33:** Ranald Mackechnie/GWR; **34/35:** 20th Century Fox, 20th Century Fox, 20th Century Fox, DreamWorks/Alamy, Alamy, Alamy, Disney/Pixar/Alamy; **36/37:** 20th Century Fox, Alamy, Alamy, Alamy, Getty, Alamy; **38/39:** Universal Pictures, Rovio/Sony Pictures, Gramercy Pictures/Alamy, Twentieth Century Fox, Allied Filmmakers; **40/41:** Paramount Pictures/Alamy, Paramount Pictures/Alamy, Science Photo Library, Theo Cohen; **42/43:** 123RF, Shutterstock, NASA, NASA, NASA, NASA, Alamy, ESO; **44/45:** NASA, 123RF, Disney/Rex, Reuters, Shutterstock, Disney; **46/47:** Fox/Alamy, Fox/Alamy, Fox/Alamy, Warner Bros/Alamy, Fox/Rex, Reuters, Fox/Alamy, Fox/Alamy, Fox/Alamy; **48/49:** Paul Michael Hughes/GWR, BBC/Alamy, BBC, BBC, BBC, Syfy; **50/51:** Disney/Alamy, Disney/Getty, Alamy, Disney/Alamy, Disney/Alamy, Paul Michael Hughes/GWR, Getty, Disney/Rex; **52/53:** Craig Ambrosio, Alamy, Disney/Getty; **54/55:** Cartoon Network, Alamy; **56/57:** Nickelodeon, Bagdasarian Productions, Disney Channel, LEGO, Alamy, Alamy, Alamy, Alamy, Alamy, Nickelodeon/Rex, Nickelodeon/Rex, Disney XD/Rex, Cartoon Network, Cartoon Network, Cartoon Network; **58/59:** Fox Searchlight, Fox Searchlight/Alamy, Lucasfilm, Walt Disney Pictures, Columbia Pictures, Fox Searchlight/Alamy, Lucasfilm, Marvel Studios/Alamy, Warner Bros, Walt Disney Pictures, Walt Disney Pictures, Walt Disney Pictures, Columbia Pictures, Warner Bros, Warner Bros/Alamy, Walt Disney Pictures/Shutterstock; **60/61:** Shutterstock, YouTube, Alamy, Alamy, Alamy, Getty, Alamy, Shutterstock; **62/63:** Alamy, Getty, Alamy, YouTube, Shutterstock; **64/65:** Paul Michael Hughes/GWR; **66/67:** Alamy, Ryan Schude/GWR, YouTube, YouTube, YouTube, Jeff Spicer; **68/69:** YouTube, Universal/Alamy, YouTube, Rex, Reddit, Mike Squires; **70/71:** YouTube; **72/73:** YouTube, YouTube, YouTube, YouTube, YouTube; **74/75:** Alamy, Getty, Getty, Alamy, Getty, Rex, Alamy, Alamy; **76/77:** Alamy, Wikipedia, Alamy, Alamy, Alamy, Alamy, Alamy, Alamy, Getty, Alamy, Alamy, Alamy; **78/79:** Alamy, Universal, YouTube, Alamy, Alamy; **80/81:** Reuters, Trevor Traynor, Getty; **82/83:** Google Unicode, Kickstarter, Shutterstock, EmojiOne, AP/PA; **84/85:** Alamy, Alamy, Alamy, NASA; **86/87:** Alamy, Getty, Alamy, Alamy, Alamy, Alamy, Rex, Alamy, iStock, Alamy, Alamy, Alamy, Alamy; **88/89:** Instagram, Kristen Stephenson/GWR; **90/91:** Twitter, Alamy, Getty, Alamy, Alamy, YouTube, Alamy, Getty, Rex, Alamy; **92/93:** Getty, Vine, Pinterest, Shutterstock, PopJam, Rex, Vine; **94/95:** YouTube, Matt Crossick/GWR, Alamy, Alamy, Rex; **96/97:** Alamy, Universal/Alamy, Disney/Alamy; **98/99:** Getty, Rex; **100/101:** Rex, Alamy, Alamy; **102/103:** Alamy, Judith Bond, Shutterstock, Walt Disney Pictures/Alamy, Stacy Jansen, Alamy; **104/105:** Alamy, Alamy, Adam White, Fotolia, Alamy, Alamy; **106/107:** Walt Disney Pictures, Village Roadshow Pictures/Shutterstock, Walt Disney Pictures; **108/109:** Warner Bros/Ronald Grant, Warner Bros/Shutterstock, Charlie Gray, Alamy, Manuel Harlan, Alamy; **110/111:** Alamy, Disney, Disney/Alamy, Joan Marcus, Rex, Alamy, Marilin Larken, Alamy, Disney, Disney, Disney/Alamy, Disney/Alamy, Alamy; **112/113:** Summit Entertainment, Alamy, Twentieth Century Fox, Lionsgate/Rex, Scholastic; **114/115:** Alamy, Alamy, Alamy, Alamy, Helen Maybanks, Alamy, Alamy, Alamy; **116/117:** Alamy, Alamy, Alamy, Alamy, Getty, Alamy, Alamy, Scholastic, Rex; **118/119:** Ranald Mackechnie/GWR; **120/121:** Alamy, Alamy, Alamy; **122/123:** Alamy, Alamy, Rex; **124/125:** Warner Bros, Bloomsbury/Alamy, Paramount Pictures/Alamy, Bloomsbury/Alamy, Disney/Alamy, Disney/Alamy, Sony Pictures/Alamy, Puffin, Warner Bros, Bloomsbury/Alamy, ITV/Rex, Penguin, Warner Bros/Alamy, Puffin, Paramount Pictures/Alamy, New Line Cinema/Alamy; **126/127:** Shutterstock, LEGO, Oculus; **128/129:** NASA, Alamy, Alamy, Press Democrat; **130/131:** Cristian Barnett/GWR; **132/133:** Paul Michael Hughes/GWR; **134/135:** Matt Alexander, Andrew Towe; **136/137:** Shutterstock; **138/139:** Alamy, Alamy, Hasbro, Sam Christmas/GWR, Alamy, Alamy, Kevin Scott Ramos/GWR, Alamy, Alamy, Alamy; **140/141:** YouTube, MCParks, Planet Minecraft, James Ellerker/GWR; **142/143:** Angelica Zander, Allemn; **144/145:** Alamy, Andrew D Bernstein/NBAE, Matt Sloan; **146/147:** Paul Michael Hughes/GWR, Pokémon; **148/149:** Ranald Mackechnie/GWR, Mattel, Mattel; **150/151:** Richard Bradbury/GWR; **152/153:** Richard Bradbury/GWR; **154/155:** Alamy, Supercell, YouTube; **156/157:** Paul Michael Hughes/GWR; **160/161:** NVIDIA, Samsung, Oculus; **162/163:** Rex, Alamy; **164/165:** James Ellerker/GWR; **166/167:** Alamy, Rex, iStock, Alamy, Alamy, Alamy; **168/169:** Alamy, Danny Moloshok, Ranald Mackechnie/GWR, Alamy, Alamy; **170/171:** Getty, Reuters, Alamy, Alamy, Guilhem Vellut; **172/173:** JoAnn Meyers; **174/175:** Columbia Pictures/Alamy, Alamy, James Ellerker/GWR, Kevin Scott Ramos/GWR, iStock; **176/177:** Getty, Getty, Getty, Alamy, Alamy, Shutterstock; **178/179:** Reuters, Getty, Alamy, Shutterstock, Shutterstock, Alamy, Getty, Getty, Getty, Shutterstock, Shutterstock; **180/181:** Danny Moloshok, Sean Litchfield; **182/183:** Martin Girard, Charles William Pelletier, Alamy, Rex, Alamy, Paul Michael Hughes/GWR, Ranald Mackechnie/GWR; **184/185:** Alamy, Getty, Jordan Sternberg, Alamy, Alamy, Reuters, Toilography, iStock, Alamy; **186/187:** Shutterstock, Mikie Farias; **188/189:** Alamy, Coasterman1234, The Curious Gnome, Reuters, Themeparkgc, Lakeyboy, Janma-Atsugatari, Jérémy-Günther-Heinz, Themeparkgc, Ivan Lucas; **190/191:** Nintendo, Alamy, Ryan Schude/GWR, Samsung, Alamy, Alamy; **192/193:** Getty, Apple, Alamy, Alamy, Bragi; **194/195:** Ryan Schude/GWR, Drew Gardner/GWR; **196/197:** Alamy, iStock, iStock, iStock, iStock, iStock; **198/199:** Alamy, Alamy, James Ellerker/GWR, Alamy, Red Bull, Paul Michael Hughes/GWR; **200/201:** Ranald Mackechnie/GWR; **202/203:** Reuters, Alamy, Stephen Lee, John Wright/GWR; **204/205:** Getty, Getty, Getty, Reuters, Lionsgate, Fox, Getty; **206/207:** Universal/Alamy, Alamy, Nintendo, Alamy, Alamy, Nickelodeon/Alamy, Sony Pictures, Rex/Marvel Studios, Warner Bros/Alamy, Alamy, Apple, Alamy; **208/209:** Paul Michael Hughes/GWR; **210/211:** Nintendo, Oculus, Nickelodeon, Nintendo, Manuel Harlan; **212/213:** DreamWorks, Universal/Alamy, Getty, Getty, Mojang; **214/215:** Universal

ACKNOWLEDGEMENTS
Juliet Barbara (Communications Director, Wikimedia Foundation); Tilman Bayer (Senior Analyst, Wikimedia Foundation); Casey Blossom (The LEGO Company); Melissa Drinkwater; e-Sports Earnings; Euromonitor International; Forbes; Justin Garvanovic (rcdb.com); Dora Howard; *Kidscreen*/Smarty Pants; Eddie Luchman; Mattel; Craig Mullaney (Facebook); musical.ly; Vipul Naik; Bruce Nash (The-Numbers.com); National Book Tokens; Nielsen; Stephanie Noon (Instagram); Gina Shalavi (Google/YouTube); SuperData; Carolyn Thomas (Facebook); VGChartz.com; Matthew White; Anne-Claire Woodfield (Nielsen BookScan)

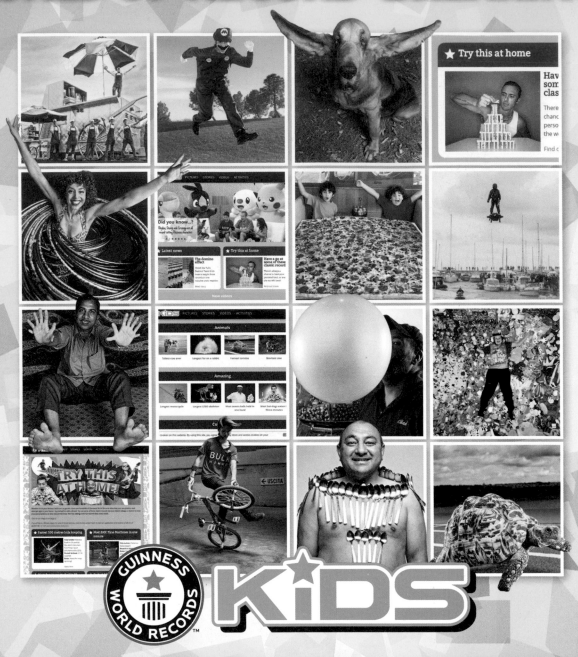